See Spot Live Longer

How to help
your dog live a longer and
healthier life!

Steve Brown & **Beth Taylor**

CREEKOBEAR PRESS

Cover photo courtesy of Charlee Bear® Dog Treats.

Drawings of Sparklin' Goldens and Charlee Bear Dogs by Beth Taylor

Printed in the United States of America

First printing, September 2004

Creekobear Press

P.O. Box 50939

Eugene, OR 97405

Cataloging-in-Publication Data

Brown, Steve and Taylor, Beth.

See Spot Live Longer, How to Help Your Dog Live a Longer, Healthier Life

p. cm.

Includes index, bibliographical references.

ISBN 0-9755306-051495

1. Dogs — nutrition

2. Dogs — health

3. Dogs — food

4. Diet and Nutrition

Library of Congress Control Number: 2004094196

Disclaimer: The information in this book is not meant to take the place of medical advice or expert veterinary care. Consult a veterinarian when there is a possibility that your dog is ill.

For Zach,
the dog who was my best friend, my constant
companion, and my business partner. Thank you, Zach,
for helping me learn how to help dogs live longer.

S.B.

For Arrow,
a perfect dog, who sent me in so many new directions,
and all the others who keep me looking for answers.

B.T.

TABLE OF CONTENTS

PART TWO: An Examination
and Comparison of the Ancestral and
Modern Diets of Dogs

PART THREE: Carcinogens and Allergens in Pet Foods

PART FOUR: Improving the Odds is Easy

PREFACE

Dogs evolved from wolves to be with people. Slowly, over tens of thousands of years, they intertwined their lives with ours. A dog becomes our best friend, our constant companion, and then dies at a young age.

I cry as I write these words. My dog of all dogs, Zach, a special mixed-breed (hybrid) called a Charlee Bear® Dog, died of cancer at age 10. I expected him to live to age 16. This book is the result of my search to discover why he died, and how I could have improved the odds that he would have lived a long healthy life.

I met many people on similar journeys of discovery, including Beth Taylor, who helped me write this book. Beth's initial focus was to find the perfect purebred dog, mine to breed the perfect hybrid. We came to the same conclusions from very different starting points. Beth and I started working together five years ago. Together, we have fed about 25,000 dogs. With this book, we'd like to help feed millions more.

Steve Brown

INTRODUCTION

Human nutrition and lifestyle studies prove there are ways to improve the odds that we will live long, healthy lives. It's simple: eat a variety of fresh, minimally-processed foods, especially fruits and vegetables; stay lean; exercise often; and avoid toxins. Good nutrition is key. Dietary habits may be instrumental in about 60% of cancers in women and about 40% in men.[1]

Good diets are just as important for dogs. The thesis of this book is that a naturally balanced raw meat, bone and vegetable-based diet ("proper raw diet") provides higher quality nutrition and fewer toxins than any dry or canned dog food diet, and therefore improves the odds that a dog will live a long, healthy life. We believe that the combination of the inappropriate macronutrient and micronutrient content of dry dog food with the inevitable toxins present in these foods is a major reason why 50% of all dogs over age ten die of cancer[2] and why cancer is the number one disease killer of dogs.[3]

We see, hear, and feel evidence of this every day. Hundreds of people, customers, friends, and veterinarians have written to us about the improvements they saw in animals in their care when the dogs (and cats) were fed a proper raw diet. Dogs stay thinner, have cleaner teeth, are more active and less achy, have fewer allergy symptoms, reduced flea problems, happier dispositions… and live longer when fed properly. In Part One we'd like to introduce you to just a few of the dogs and cats we've known whose lives have been transformed by a change of diet.

To feed dogs properly, we must break through the myths propagated by decades of advertisements by the big pet food companies. Myths such as "never change your dog's diet," "never give the dog table scraps," and "dry dog food is all your dog needs to eat" are almost folklore, and wrong. In order to prove to the discriminating reader that these myths are false, the second and third parts of this book are detailed and well-documented.

In Part Two we compare the macronutrient (protein, carbohydrate, fat, water) and micronutrient (vitamins, minerals, antioxidants, enzymes) content of the ancestral diet with that of the modern diet of dogs. We'll see that the ancestral diet consisted of a variety of raw, high protein, low carbohydrate, and high-bacterial content foods with natural sources of micronutrients, including cancer-fighting antioxidants. This is almost the exact opposite of the modern diet of dogs.

In Part Three we present strong evidence that the low cost ingredients used in dry dog foods contain potent toxins and allergens, and that the high temperature cooking used to mass-produce dry pet foods create potent carcinogens (substances that cause cancer).

In Part Four, "Improving The Odds is Easy," we give specific, easy-to-follow advice about diet, avoidance of toxins, exercise, and keeping dogs lean that will help improve the odds that dogs will live longer.

In the appendices, we present the cost structure of typical dry foods, with and without human-edible meats; Beth gives advice on how to choose a commercial dry dog food; Steve discusses "the riddle of missing hybrid vigor;" and we explore the question of whether the health problems of dogs are primarily genetic, "womb effect" or from the environment (including diet) after birth.

You can effectively use this book by simply using Part Four as a guideline for improving the diet of your dogs. However, one of our goals in writing this book is to make the scientific information in Parts Two and Three accessible to all, so that the reader would be able to understand why we're making our recommendations, and then be able to expose others to this information, helping to feed many more dogs properly.

We hope this book helps your Spot live a longer, healthier life. We promise you that we will continue to learn from our experiences feeding dogs and from our continued research, and will report new information on our web site, www.seespotlivelonger.com.

p.s. The information in this book is especially important if you're getting a puppy or have a pregnant dog.

PART ONE
Food Makes a Difference

"All processed pet foods… are missing something that seems to… be the most important "nutrient" of all. This key ingredient is practically ignored by nutritional scientists, but we can occasionally sense its presence. It is a quality found only in freshly grown, uncooked whole food: Life Energy!" —*Richard Pitcairn, DVM*

CHAPTER 1
Cases From Our Files

We talk to many people about dogs and diets. We speak with our customers, retailers, dog people, cat people, and veterinarians. The Internet brings us more. Many people are distraught by the illness of a beloved companion. We try to help them all.

In this process, our lives are punctuated by stories like the ones that follow. The animals we hear about don't all live and thrive. Almost all of them are helped. Their stories remind us daily of the amazing results we can get by respecting what food has to offer, the results we may experience through feeding our animals a diet that's appropriate for their body, helping the body to do what it is so well designed to do; stay splendidly healthy.

The stories that follow were chosen to illustrate some of the major areas in which ill health is common in dogs. We've included a couple of cat stories even though this is a book primarily about dogs. The symptoms and illnesses in cats are somewhat different but the causes are the same. Some of these animals came to our attention because they were fed foods that we developed. We heard about others through veterinarians who recommend fresh food diets as part of their integrative approach to medicine.

As you read, you may be reminded of your dog. Or you may be reminded of a dog who is no longer alive. Many of us frequently think about how we could have helped those dogs if we knew what we know now. It's true, we could have. They are the dogs and cats who taught us enough to be looking now for the information in this book and others.

It is our desire to do better for our animals and for yours, now and in the future, that drove us to write this book. We all do the best we can. Today we know a lot more about what dogs, cats and humans need to be healthy than we did even 5 years ago, and we have a much better chance of keeping our animals and ourselves healthy.

The memories of the animals we learned with are precious, and those dogs and cats do not blame us for what we didn't know.

Enjoy these stories as much as we do, and please send us yours!

TESSA: Another Golden with Allergies and Hot Spots

I thought that if I found a genetically perfect puppy, I'd have a healthy dog. I found my perfect puppy, with healthy parents and all possible clearances, a beautiful Golden Retriever. I fed her the "best" dry food, the one the breeder recommended, after much research on my own. When Tessa was two, she began to show the "typical" signs of allergies so common in the breed: skin infections, hot spots, and seasonal allergies. By the time she was 5 she was dependent on steroids and antibiotics. I was increasingly aware of the dangers involved in long-term use of these therapies, but the hot spots and skin infections had to be treated. Tessa was beautiful, athletic, energetic, and ill. Was the breeder lying?

My veterinarians had never felt that food and nutrition were a big factor in health. For myself, I was clear that humans needed a variety of fresh food for health; why not dogs? I thought I found some of the problems in dry food, and moved toward human-edible ingredients, no corn, better meats. Tessa got better. I added green supplements and vitamins and oils to help with symptoms. As I learned more, it became more important to find the tools for the whole body to work together instead of suppressing symptoms, to find the right raw materials to fuel a healthy immune system. Though Tessa was better, we were still using steroids and antibiotics. I started to question the basics: why was I feeding my dog grains at all? What if there were no "evil ingredients", and the problem had more to do with just the wrong ingredients? Gradually I incorporated fresh food into Tessa's diet and immediately saw a radical improvement.

After two years of a mostly raw diet, at 8, Tessa was down to a couple of hot spots a year, which I could care for with bathing alone. Then I took the last of the dry food away. By this time Tessa was 9.

Within 2 months I saw a level of health and vitality in her that had never been present before. It took several years for Tessa to heal.

For the last 3 years of her life, Tessa was completely healthy, a vibrant, rowdy, loud being who took great joy in life. It was a great joy for me to finally have some answers to the "normal" conditions all around me, for me to be able to help others find better health for their animals.

BOBBY: Oozing, Balding, and Listless

Bobby was sad, smelly, bald, and listless—and just a pup. His eyes were swollen; his muzzle and legs red and inflamed. He was continually on antibiotics, steroids, and anti-diarrhea medication. He was eating an excellent quality dry "health food for dogs". Weekly vet visits were routine. Donna was seriously considering ending Bobby's life. His misery was never ending, his medical care very expensive, and there seemed to be no hope that current treatment would be effective.

Through searching for options for Bobby, Donna found a holistic veterinarian in her area whose practice focuses on food as a starting point to health. The veterinarian recommended a fresh food diet. Bobby's diet is now a meat-based diet with vegetables. He has doubled in size, grown a beautiful coat, and is totally drug free. He's described as a bundle of energy.

Donna sent some photos to her veterinarian with this note: "I hope that these photographs will inspire others to step up to the challenge of opening their minds and looking past traditional beliefs to truly do what is best for their pets" —*from the files of Karen Shaw Becker, DVM NMD*

ELI: Skin Infections and Deep Sores

Eli, a beautiful Golden Retriever, was 8 years old when things got really bad. He had occasional "hot spots" and itching, and minor skin problems, which went away on their own, but his people didn't think it was serious. It didn't interfere with his life as "good buddy and real goof." Then he started to lose the hair on his face and tail. Large sores appeared on his legs. Medicated baths were suggested and this advice was followed for a few weeks with no improvement. Eli's folks looked for a second opinion. Their first veterinarian told them that he felt that these were the first outward signs of some form of cancer, and to have a good time with Eli while they could.

Like so many people, Eli's folks found a holistic veterinarian in the hope of saving their friend's life. They were lucky to find one with experience in fresh food diets. She felt that food was the place to start. Michelle and John were taken aback by the raw components of the diet but after a few days of discussion decided they had nothing to lose.

It wasn't the first stages of cancer. Eli's coat started to grow back in two or three weeks. The sores took longer to heal. They were very deep and it was several months before they were completely gone. When I met Eli he still had a rat tail and I could see the remains of the deep, oozing sores on his legs, but by that time they were small pink patches. John says: "He eats with tremendous gusto. We have to spend time making his food. We even have to walk him and play with him! Pretty cool!" Within 6 months there was no sign that Eli had ever been in ill health. His coat was lush. His hot spots and "itchies" never returned.

Dogs with "allergies" might experience this spectacular healing. Sometimes they don't. Sometimes their immune systems are not able to recover completely, as did Eli and Tessa, the other Golden in this section. The healing may take years, as it did with Tessa, every season showing less need to depend on immune suppressants like Prednisone and antihistamines. Any improvement that allows the body to work better on its own is, in our opinions, worth doing even if there is not total healing.

This story is not unusual. For hundreds of dogs we know, eating fresh food has resulted in total health. —*from the files of Karen Shaw Becker, DVM NMD*

MISTY: Allergies

Misty was only 3. She's a black Labrador Retriever who has had "allergy" problems all her life. Her sister, Molly, is healthy. Misty suffered from allergy symptoms all year. Misty's caretaker, Dawn, has a medical background and had consulted several veterinarians looking for solutions for Misty's problems. They all recommended the same thing: Prednisone and antihistamines. Even with these drugs, Misty scratched herself bloody. She had no hair on her hindquarters. Misty's intense scratching frequently interrupted the family's sleep. She drank a lot of water due to the steroids. Expensive prescription foods from the veterinarian did not help. A dermatologist recommended testing and allergy shots.

Dawn's sister had been suggesting for some time that Dawn consult her holistic veterinarian. Dawn is a RN who didn't have much faith in holistic medicine, but by this time she was willing to give it a try. Misty started on a fresh food diet on August 1st, and by August 10th was medication free. By September 5th Misty had almost all her hair back and had lost 6 pounds of the weight caused by the Prednisone.

Dawn is more interested in "holistic" solutions now, and tells her friends about fresh diets for their dogs. —*from the files of Karen Shaw Becker, DVM NMD*

BO: Chronic Skin Problems

Bo, a frisky 10 year old Bichon, is having a great time despite almost total blindness caused by the steroids used to control his chronic skin problems, which were attributed to food allergies. He has never been very interested in food, though there was some improvement in his appetite after his family switched him to a better dry food.

Bo had spent much of his time with his hair shaved. He chewed his feet until they bled, and had frequent hot spots. His whole body was itchy. Two years ago, during the worst of the allergy season, Debbie tried to switch Bo to fresh food. Any change has been difficult for Bo, and he wasn't able to handle the switch at that time. The slightest change caused vomiting. When his immune system was a little more settled in the spring, Debbie was able to switch Bo with no difficulty. He immediately began to feel better, bouncing around like a Bichon should. Debbie weaned him off the steroids and antihistamines that had made his life bearable.

For the past year and a half, Bo has had no allergy symptoms (except when Debbie was unable to get the fresh food diet she had been feeding him). Now that he is back on only fresh food, with no grains at all, he is fine. His coat grew back quickly, and he no longer needs to be shaved. He's still almost blind, but he doesn't know it.

Debbie wrote to us: "Bo LOVES his food! I highly recommend this food to all dog owners! Why wait until your dog is sick? I truly believe that most dogs were never intended to eat the highly processed foods with grain added. Bo's (commercially-prepared fresh food diet) may be more costly but we have saved lots of money by not having to buy medications constantly for Bo. Bo is a lot happier not being drugged and uncomfortable. I wish we had known about this years ago!"

There are times when steroid drugs are lifesavers. All veterinarians are aware that the long-term effects of ongoing use will shorten the life of an animal. Once they are no longer needed, and once the cause of the body's inappropriate response is removed, dog's (and cat's and human's) bodies have a chance to return to normal functioning. The return to normal may take some time. Given how bad Bo's skin problems were, how long he'd been on the drugs, how difficult it was to change his diet, we thought it would take time for him to show major improvement. Every dog is different. Bo healed very fast.

It's uncommon in our experience for dogs to have digestive difficulty switching diets as long as things are taken slowly. It seems that in cases where it's so clear that fresh food is needed, sometimes it's necessary to go VERY slowly. In Bo's case, it was more a matter of choosing a time when there were fewer stressors on his system.

RUDY: "Liver Disease"?

Rudy was 12 when he got sick. He was always hungry, but vomited food and even ice cubes. Blood tests showed elevated liver enzymes and an enlarged liver. The vets that Tim and Monica consulted gave them no hope for any treatment or improvement. Many people would have concluded that their dog had lived a pretty long time and ended Rudy's life. He was sick and unable to eat, and would have died soon in any case. Instead, Tim and Monica went on a "last-resort" search for other possible treatment. They found a holistic veterinarian who reviewed Rudy's file and told them that not only was Rudy's "time not up", but that he had a good chance of living a few more years through a change of diet and some supplements.

Rudy recovered.

Monica says: "Two and a half years later, at the age of 15, Rudy continues to amaze us. His new 'lease on life' though this natural managed care has opened a whole world of possibilities for all of us."

—*from the files of Karen Shaw Becker, DVM NMD*

CHEYENNE: Mast Cell Cancer

Cheyenne is a 5-year-old chow/cocker mix. She had been diagnosed with Mast Cell Cancer, stage III: three tumors had been removed. Julie, her human, did a great deal of research on the topic and found that the prognosis was grim. While researching, Julie also found information on the effects diet—specifically raw foods—can have on the immune system and a dog's natural ability to fight cancer.

Julie had fed Cheyenne a high quality commercial dry dog food since she was a puppy. What she read convinced her that she was feeding the cancer. Within 3 weeks of surgery, one of the tumors had grown back. An oncologist gave Cheyenne 2 months to live without Chemotherapy, 6–8 months with Chemotherapy.

Quality of time or quantity of time? Julie opted for quality, and decided against Chemotherapy. She changed Cheyenne's diet to an all raw meat-based diet. Within one month of the diet change, the tumor, which had grown back, was gone. There have been no signs of any spread of the cancer. We first heard about Cheyenne early in 2002. When we checked recently, Cheyenne was still doing fine! Julie says: "Cheyenne feels good and her appetite is great. She loves to chase squirrels and bunnies and runs all the time. Every day is a gift—she's my best friend!"

Fresh food might not cure your dog's mast cell tumors. They are hard to remove surgically and often recur. Julie's story, however, is one of many that we have heard in which radical improvement was seen. Sometimes tumors are removed surgically and do not recur, but in this case the tumor was already back. Julie knows the connection between her active, happy dog and the fresh food diet she is using. —*from the files of Karen Shaw Becker, DVM NMD*

COOPER: Smelly Ears, Fat, Flaky, and Arthritic

Cooper, a chocolate Labrador, had a hard start in life, recovering from what was probably Parvo through the use of intensive antibiotics and IV fluids. Possibly as a result of the interventions that saved his life, Cooper had smelly, infected ears most of the time. He had pimples on his muzzle and occasionally elsewhere, which were treated with more antibiotics. His coat was dull and very flaky. These things didn't slow him down much. He was a survivor with a taste for whole bottles of Vaseline (jar included) and 2-pound bags of chocolate. Cooper was fed a grocery store dry food, and had the "usual" vaccinations and conventional medical treatment. As Cooper grew older, he started to have a lot of trouble with pain from arthritis and weakness in one of his back legs. The pain was treated with Rimadyl. The smelly ears were constant, he had large amounts of tartar on his teeth, and he was overweight.

The last chocolate episode resulted in a six-day intensive care stay. When Cooper was released, he was so weak he needed to be supported to walk. At this point, his family decided to try a fresh food diet to see if the quality of Cooper's life could be improved.

Three months later, Cooper's coat sparkled. His ears were clean for the first time in his life. The tartar on his teeth was much improved, and eventually disappeared completely. He lost weight, and his original lean, muscled build emerged. One back leg continued to give him trouble, but the rest of his aches and pains disappeared. His appetite for inappropriate items continued, but his "counter-surfing" habits became much less obsessive. For the last three years of Cooper's life, he felt a lot better than he did during the first 10.

This is a story we hear very often. Cooper actually felt much better for most of his life than many dogs with these problems. We're so used to our fat Cockers with smelly ears and our fat Labradors with arthritis that it is really a stretch to imagine that it could be different. It does not occur to many of us that food might be an alternative to dangerous drugs. In our experience, these are some of the most obvious and dramatic problems alleviated by food—and the changes are immediate. The ears, the pain, and the fat are sometimes history within weeks. Improvement is often seen in a few days.

BJ: Old, Inflamed, and Immobile

BJ is a very elderly mini dachshund. Most would say "How could you do any better than this?" At 17, he had a number of chronic problems that were considered part of old age. His teeth were encrusted with tartar, and he smelled pretty bad. He had a large abscess on his cheek that came and went, and was quite painful. His coat was sticky, patchy and matted, partly because he would allow nobody to groom him. BJ had eaten average commercial food all his life. He was fairly cheerful as long as you didn't try to touch him. His back end did not work very well, but in a dachshund that old, it was amazing that it worked at all.

Connie consulted a veterinary chiropractor to see if BJ might be able to have better use of his back legs. It was suggested that Connie try either switching to a fresh food diet for BJ or supplementing his dry food with fresh food to help alleviate arthritic inflammation. Connie started by supplementing with fresh food. Within a few weeks the abscess on his cheek was radically better and the tartar was much reduced. He loved his food, and Connie switched over all the way to fresh food. When BJ started treatment, he was so stiff he could not turn his head, but after a few weeks on fresh food he was feeling better. His coat is shiny. The abscess has not returned. BJ's flexible enough now to bite people trying to help him, but he is not so inclined to try. BJ is well over 19 now. His back end is not perfect, but he can cover ground at a good pace when he wants too. Mealtime is certainly one of those occasions.

RASCAL: Seizures

Rascal, a Chesapeake Bay Retriever, is 5 years old with a 3-year history of seizures. She had been on the anticonvulsants Phenobarbital and potassium bromide for years, but still had frequent seizures. Rascal's veterinarian recommended that Rascal change over to a raw food diet. Within a few days, she became very lethargic and her back legs were very wobbly. The owner took Rascal to the vet where they tested her blood levels of Phenobarbital and potassium bromide. It was discovered that they were dangerously high.

The frightened owner lowered the medication and put Rascal back on the dry food diet. Rascal improved. The owner attempted to feed Rascal a raw food diet and the same events occurred. Rascal's holistic veterinarian concluded that the raw foods, rich in enzymes and proteins, etc. enhanced the absorption of the medicines. The dosages of both medications were gradually decreased, while continuing to feed the raw diet. Rascal is currently seizure free! —*from the files of Julie Mayer, DVM*

PEBBLES AND BAMBAM: Feline Infectious Peritonitis

Pebbles and Bam Bam are two young kittens diagnosed with Feline Infectious Peritonitis or FIP. They never had formed healthy stools, had chronic eye and nose discharge, and had upper respiratory symptoms. Occasionally they were too sick to eat. Their veterinarian, Dr.

Julie Mayer, prescribed supplements designed to help the immune system with glandulars and herbs. They improved somewhat. It wasn't until the owner changed the diet to raw food that their stools became normal. Within two weeks, they gained weight, their eyes cleared, and their coats improved. *—from the files of Julie Mayer, DVM*

SWEETS: Inflammatory Bowel Disease

Sweets, a 4-year-old domestic shorthaired cat, was diagnosed with Inflammatory Bowel Disease. She was on high doses of steroids to regulate the bowel movements and to decrease vomiting and to increase appetite. She was also on a prescription dry food diet for intestinal problems. The owner wanted to get Sweets off the steroids. Her veterinarian recommended a raw diet and within two months Sweets was weaned off the medication without any problems. To this day Sweets is off medication and she loves her food! *—from the files of Julie Mayer, DVM*

THE LHASAS: Ears, Itching, Hot Spots

Two young adult Lhasas from the same family had skin allergies. They had severe itching, hot spots, chronic ear infections, and a foul odor for years. Their vet tried many different medications and dry foods. Nothing helped. During a holistic consultation, Dr. Mayer advised the family to serve a home made diet with plenty of fish and omega 3 fatty acids and a digestive enzyme. Within one month, the skin on both dogs completely cleared up. The dogs felt better, smelled better and had more energy. *—from the files of Julie Mayer, DVM*

HAANY: Dachsie-Mazing Weight Loss!

Chuck's 13-year-old Dachshund, Haany, was irritable, achy, and quite overweight. Chuck had been having great success losing weight on the Atkins diet. One day, Chuck took a look at Haany and thought, "Well, if it works for me, what about the dog?" He contacted us and started feeding Haany and his companion, Kipper (a 4 year old Dachshund) our commercial raw diet in October of 2002. At that time, Haany was always hungry and Kipper was not interested in food. Haany was pretty hefty, with a belly barely clearing the floor. In January, Haany was 5 pounds lighter, no longer acted like he was starving and was much more cheerful. Kipper was much more interested in food, had lost a couple of pounds (though Chuck had not felt he was overweight) and was feeling terrific.

DOLLY: Not Quite The End of the Road

This letter came to us from Randi Berger, who runs a rescue organization:

I've had a dog rescue agency since 1987, Recycled Pets, which specializes in helping many senior dogs who have lost their homes.

In early 2000 a very old Shih Tzu was abandoned in a crate on the porch of one of our foster homes. She was depressed and angry; not adoptable. She became one of our beloved family members. Dolly slowly came out of her depression. She was a feisty, tenacious little girl who acted like a puppy, although she looked 100 years old. She bounced around the house dominating all of the other dogs and we all admired her resiliency in overcoming her late-life transition.

Early this year, only 3 years since she entered our lives, Dolly became very weak, disoriented, and rapidly lost a lot of weight. Blood work showed nothing abnormal and the consensus from several different vets was to put her to sleep. I have always valued the life of a senior dog the most, and believe that they deserve as much time being honored and cherished as possible. Although Dolly became quite feeble, spending most of her life sleeping, she still was enjoying food. Dolly's strength was vacillating over the months. I decided that if she stopped eating, then I would agree with my staff that she had no quality of life.

In September of '03, Dolly stopped eating. I tried to entice her with anything and everything.. Her body seemed tired beyond repair and her feistiness was now a part of her past. This time, if I entered a veterinary clinic holding Dolly, I would be leaving without her. I had picked up a bag of your (frozen raw diet produced by the authors) food and was testing it on some of our other picky 4-legged eaters. It was late afternoon, and Dolly had not awakened that day. While offering some of your food to 7 of our very spoiled 4-legged ones, I put a frozen cube in front of Dolly's nearly comatose face. She popped her little head up, and grabbed it from my hand. Although she was weak, she had enough sense to stare at me after finishing it, demanding I give her another cube. It took her quite a while to eat each cube, but she managed to polish off about 5 more cubes. An hour later, she had the strength to go to the bathroom outside on her own and after, was hungry for more food. Dolly slept peacefully through the night and awoke in the morning hungry. I phoned the veterinary office to tell them I would not be bringing her in.

Days later, she is more alert and has started walking again on her own. She is regaining the strength we thought we would never see again. What happened with Dolly and your food is remarkable and like nothing else I have ever seen from a food, supplement, medication, potion, therapy, etc. I feel that the world needs to know the potential that this food has to save the lives of other dogs that may be written off as beyond hope. If it did this for a dog who had such little life left in her, we can only imagine what it may prevent in the lives of healthy, normal dogs.

No one ever really knows when our time is up here, but each extra day that Dolly was given because of this food is a gift to us all.

Look for Randi Berger's upcoming book, *My Recycled Pets, Diary of a Dog Addict.* It can be ordered at Randi's website, www.recycledpetsrescue.com.

CHAPTER 2
Talk to Your Veterinarian

If you spend any time with dogs or cats you are acquainted with individuals with health problems similar to the ones we have discussed here. Some of these problems are life threatening. They need the supervision of a veterinarian. If you have a dog or cat with serious problems, we urge you to seek the help of a veterinarian with fresh food experience.

If your dog is diabetic and on medication, or has kidney or liver issues, has heart problems and is on medication (as well as many other conditions), you must have medical supervision as you change over to a raw meat-based diet. Medication dosages are likely to change, and close monitoring will be needed. The dog with seizures we talked about earlier is a good example of the need for medical supervision.

Our book is not designed to take the place of a one-to-one relationship with a veterinarian: it is designed to help you learn so that you can make more informed choices for your animals and yourself.

CHAPTER 3
But My Dog is Perfectly Healthy!

As we wrote the chapter about the wonderful improvements in ill dogs and cats after being fed proper fresh food diets, we understood more fully that our true challenge with this book is encouraging people whose dogs are healthy to start feeding fresh foods now, before their dogs become ill.

If we wait until there is a problem, a return to health may not be possible despite the amazing recuperative resources of our bodies and those of our animals.

If we want our dogs to be healthy tomorrow, we need to provide their bodies with the proper tools today. Even if we are unable to do this perfectly, an effort to include as much whole, unprocessed food as possible in our animal's diets will lay the foundation for health in the future and do much to help the body deal with any current problems.

PART TWO
An Examination and
Comparison
of the Ancestral and Modern
Diets of Dogs

In this part we're going to examine the ancestral diet —the only natural diet—of the dog. We'll see that the ancestral diet consisted of a variety of raw, high protein, low carbohydrate, and high bacterial content foods with natural sources of micronutrients, including cancer-fighting antioxidants. This is almost the exact opposite of the modern diet of dogs, who eat the same dry dog food everyday. We'll see how we can easily correct this and feed dogs more natural diets in Part Four of this book.

The Natural Diet of Dogs

Variety
of raw, real foods teeming with bacteria

Macronutrients
low in carbohydrate, high in protein, high in fat, high water content

Micronutrients
whole, naturally sourced vitamins and minerals, full range of antioxidants and enzymes

CHAPTER 4
Foods That Made the Dog

Bones, pieces of carcass, rotten greens and fruit,
fish guts, discarded seed and grains, animal guts and heads,
some uneaten human food and wastes....[1]

"The staple diet of carnivores living
in a natural setting includes other animals, carrion,
and occasionally fruits and grasses."[2]

What a successful species dogs have been! Dogs evolved from wolves, probably about 14,000 years ago in East Asia.[3] The prevailing opinion among scientists is that the wolf is the principal, if not the only ancestor of the dog,[4] and has existed for more than 5 million years.[5] Continually adapting to human societies, often living on the discarded waste products of humans, dogs have thrived. The fittest dogs, those best able to find food and utilize the nutrients in their diets, reproduced. For almost 14,000 years, the dogs' bodies, brains, dental structure and digestive system structure (gut morphology) evolved to best utilize their ancestral diet. Anatomically, the digestive system of the domestic dog is still very similar to those of feral carnivores.[6]

There is very little debate about this. At the Iams International Nutrition Symposium, 1996, Dr. Buddington of Mississippi State University stated: "Comparative studies have revealed a close relationship between intestinal characteristics, the evolutionary diet, and requirements of energy and nutrients." His paper considered how "intestinal characteristics reflect patterns of gene expression that are related to each species evolutionary diet." He goes on to say, "during a species evolution, intestinal characteristics adapt to match the natural diet."[7]

Dogs have eaten their natural diet for 14,000 to 5,000,000 years, depending upon how one defines the difference between dogs and wolves. Dogs have eaten dry dog foods (Science Diet,® Iams,® Solid Gold,® Nutro,® Ol' Roy,® Innova,® Nature's Recipe,® etc) for less than 100 years. Commercial dog foods were first introduced in 1860, but did not become popular until Purina developed the extrusion process in 1957. For 99.995 to 99.999% of the canine species existence, dogs have eaten their natural, ancestral diet. For only 0.005% of their history, they've eaten dry dog foods.

Indeed, Ray and Lorna Coppinger, in their recent, well-researched, groundbreaking book *Dogs: A Startling New Understanding of Canine Origin, Behavior & Evolution* show that throughout the world there are still millions of non-domesticated dogs eating, for the most part, discarded human foods (including fish guts and human wastes) and carrion. The Coppingers also show that many of our purebred dogs are just a few generations away from the non-domesticated village and sheep dogs that thrived on their natural diet.[9]

CHAPTER 5
A Variety of Raw, Real Foods Teeming with Microbes

Canine Gourmet Dining: Carrion
"The dead and putrefying flesh of an animal."
About 100,000,000,000,000,000,000
bacteria per ounce, some friendly, some not.

We all know humans need to eat a variety of foods. Imagine the health problems we would have if we ate the same food every day, week after week, all of our lives. This is true with dogs as well. Like us, they need to eat a variety of foods. This is not what most of us have been taught. It is well documented that people may become sensitive to foods they eat most often.[1] The same is true for dogs. Dr. Lowell Ackerman, a prominent canine dermatologist, wrote, "Dogs (and people) can become allergic to foods they have eaten repeatedly, whether it is beef, soy, lamb—or strawberries."[2] Innovative Veterinary Diets wrote, in a newsletter to veterinarians, "Not surprisingly, the foods most commonly associated with ARF (adverse reactions to food) are those fed most often."[3] Dr. Patricia White, a prominent practicing allergy veterinarian agreed, stating, at the 2003 Western Veterinary Conference: "The most common ingredient causing food allergy is the one that is consumed most often."[4] In a brochure about their hypoallergenic veterinary diet dog food, 2003, the Nestle Purina Company said "It has been estimated that food hypersensitivity may contribute to pruritus (itching) in up to 62% of dogs."[5]

We've been told that if we change a dog's food, the dog may have gastrointestinal (GI) problems such as loose stools or diarrhea. This is true, to some extent. If one quickly changes the food of a dog that has never had dietary variety, the dog may get an upset stomach and have GI problems. When this happens, the outdated thinking that change and variety are undesirable is reinforced, and the myth that dogs should eat the same food every day of their lives is perpetuated. Just imagine if you only ate processed cereal (fortified with all the vitamins and minerals you need) every day, every meal, your entire life. Then you were introduced to real foods, and ate a steak, fresh broccoli and a salad for the first time in your life. You, too, would have a GI problem.

Just as with people, when dogs get accustomed to variety, it's the only way they want to eat. Dogs, given a choice, want to eat a variety of foods.[6] An animal behaviorist for Waltham, one of the largest dog food companies in the world (owned by the Mars candy bar people), stated: "Clearly, just as in humans, sensory variety enhances the motivation to feed."[7] It is especially important to feed puppies a variety-based diet. Some dogs, and many cats, if fed just one food for many years, especially when young, may get fixed on one particular flavor and reject new foods.

Feeding your dog a variety of foods helps ensure that the dog receives all the micronutrients she needs and helps reduce your dog's exposure to high-levels of any one type of toxin, including arsenic and specific mycotoxins.[8] For example, high levels of arsenic have been reported in young, commercially raised (not organic) chickens by researchers from the National Institute of Health and the U.S.D.A..[9] While the researchers believe that the high levels of arsenic are not a problem for most humans who eat a variety-based diet, we know many dogs who eat a commercial chicken-based food everyday. We are concerned about these dogs' long-term exposure to arsenic. Mycotoxins, the waste products from molds that eat grains, may be a major factor in canine cancer. Dogs who eat dry food may be exposed to these toxins also on a daily basis. We'll discuss this in more detail in Chapter 11.

A typical week of meals for our dogs includes commercially-prepared raw diets—chicken, turkey, ostrich, and beef-based—warm raw eggs, raw whole turkey necks, raw beef, ostrich and buffalo bones, avocado skins, nuts and canned sardines. Lots of variety, composed of unprocessed, uncooked whole foods.

REAL, RAW FOODS

The dog's natural diet consisted of real, raw foods. Real foods are the foods we find at farmer's markets. Real foods occur in nature, and usually spoil unless kept refrigerated or frozen. This is quite different from the dry ingredients used in most extruded dog foods: meat meals, grains and human-made vitamins and minerals. Many dry dog food manufacturing plants have no refrigerators or freezers, except in the lunchroom for the human staff. All the ingredients they use are powders and come in bags. Even the oils and fats they use do not require refrigeration because they contain powerful preservatives.

We all know raw foods are important for humans. Many scientific studies have shown that raw forms of fruits and vegetables are most consistently associated with lower risks of cancer.[10] We believe that raw foods are just as important for dogs, who never developed the habit of cooking their foods.

Until the advent of inexpensive commercial dog foods, we believe that most household dogs ate raw meats and other raw foods. Dr. Clive McCay of Cornell University, author of what may be the last independent (not associated with a large petfood company) nutrition textbook used in veterinary schools, *Nutrition of the Dog* (1944), stated: "The cooking of meat for dogs is a waste of time from the point of view of nutrition. Cooking tends to destroy vitamins. In fact, the meat meals commonly used in dog feeds are often so overheated in processing that they are devoid of the important vitamin B1."[11] He also states: "raw meat is probably the best digested protein."[12] Ironically, Dr. McCay's book, written in 1943, during World War II, when animal protein was scarce, appears to be a defense of the then radical idea of using carbohydrates in dog food.

Cooking reduces the potency of almost all nutrients and completely destroys some nutrients.[13,14,15,16] Essential nutrients particularly susceptible to high heat include thiamin, niacin, folic acid, vitamin C, and pantothenic acid.[17] Even blanching significantly reduces antioxidant activity of foods.[18] The higher the temperature and the higher the pressure, the greater the loss of nutrients.[19] When foods are cooked, some micronutrients are affected more than others, which changes the natural balance of micronutrients. Please see the micronutrient section in Chapter 7, for a more thorough discussion.

Many commercial dog foods use meat meals. Meat meals are the rendered products from mammal tissues. What remains after the fat has been drawn off is dried, and the resulting meal is almost all protein. Processing of the meat meal reduces protein quality. Meat meal used in dog foods is cooked twice: first to make the meal, and then to make the dog food itself.

The vast majority of dry pet foods sold are made by the extrusion process. This process is extremely efficient: modern extruders can produce up to 50,000 pounds of petfood an hour! The process involves mixing all the ingredients together to form a dough, which is then cooked in an extruder and forced through a die under high pressure (600–700 psi) and high temperature (300–400ºF). This is a much harsher process on nutrients than baking in your oven at home. Articles in pet food industry magazines acknowledge this:

"Extrusion is considered the most aggressive process against vitamins."[20]

"Antioxidant losses of 50–80% through these high temperature, high pressure processes."[21]

Pet food recipes anticipate some potency losses and compensate by adding 20 to 25 different human-synthesized, pure-compound forms of vitamins and minerals, often sprayed on the food after extrusion.

There are thousands of different micronutrients in natural foods, both known and unknown. In order to feed our dogs a diet with the full range and balance of natural antioxidants and other micronutrients, the diet must be, for the most part, raw.

High temperature cooking not only destroys nutrition, it also can create potent carcinogens called Heterocyclic Amines, discussed in Chapter 10. High temperature cooking does kill bacteria. This may not be a good thing. Dogs evolved eating lots of bacteria.

Why Dogs Can Eat Carrion. Dogs live in a bacterial world. Dogs are scavengers. They eat just about anything that has calories, including carrion, raw fish guts and feces. They live in a world of germs. In one gram (about $1/28$ of an ounce) of soil there may be 500 million bacteria, and nearly 1 million fungi, in addition to nearly 500,000 multi-cellular animals like nematodes.[22] In one gram of fertile soil, in our gardens, there may be as many as 10^{10} microbes.[23] There can easily be as many bacteria in a drop of water as there are humans on earth.

We live in a world dominated by bacteria: it is estimated that bacteria represent, collectively,[24] a mass equivalent to that of all trees and other plants combined. Indeed recent studies suggest that the mass of bacteria existing below the ground may be larger than the mass of all living things, including bacteria, at the earth's surface.[25]

The dog goes out for a walk. She walks on dirt, and a few grams stick to her pads. She comes in and licks her pads. She consumes about a billion bacteria, perhaps hundreds of different species. No problem. The dog's digestive system is accustomed to many species of bacteria in large numbers.

> In one gram of soil,
> there are 1 billion germs,
> 500,000 multi-cellular animals....
>
> And the dog licks her pads.

Dogs eat dead animals and carrion. A dead animal's meat quickly acquires a high bacterial load, from the saliva (a billion microbes per gram) of the predators, from the digestive tracts of insects, from its own gut (about one trillion bacteria per gram in the colon in a live animal)[26] and perhaps even from a bacteria that may have killed the animal. In warm climates, bacteria consuming the meat grow rapidly, with most types of E. coli doubling every twenty minutes.[27] This is exponential growth. The dog consumes a huge number of bacteria, often from the guts of animals, which may contain many species that can seriously harm humans. "All of us harbor in our colons something like five hundred species of potentially deadly organisms."[28] These organisms are rarely a problem for the dog.

Closer to home, think of the dog burying a bone, and then digging it up weeks later and eating it. The number of bacteria on that bone is a number beyond our comprehension. A quadrillion x 10^{10} may not be an exaggeration.

Live bacteria are certainly of nutritional benefit for the dog. Consuming live bacteria may help the dog develop healthy, diverse gut flora. In humans, researchers have recently found that some infectious strains of *E. coli* stifle the growth of cancerous intestinal cells.[29] Humans did not evolve on sterile, bacteria-free foods any more than dogs did.

In addition, the authors believe (with, at this time, not a lot of scientific documentation) that live bacteria and the inevitable bacteriophages (viruses that eat bacteria), as foods, may be highly nutritious for dogs. Live bacteria and bacteriophages provide protein. Live bacteria are also a source of adenosine triphosphate (ATP). ATP is the universal conveyer of energy in all living cells, from bacteria to plants to animals. All forms of biological work are powered by the splitting of ATP. When the dog eats live bacteria, the dog consumes ATP. It has been established that when bacterial cells are killed, the ATP disappears.[30] The dog's ancestral diet contained copious amounts of ATP, the modern diet contains very little.

Almost all dry dog foods contain small amounts of bacteria. The extrusion process significantly reduces the bacterial population, but does not eliminate it.[31] For example, a 1995 study found that 83% of 40 dog foods tested contained the bacteria *Bacillus cereus*, and 25% contained *Enterococcus faecalis* (a sign of contamination by fecal material).[32] A 1964 study found *Salmonella*, of seventeen different serotypes, in 27% of tested dry dog foods.[33]

Throughout the dog's long evolutionary history, those dogs that were able to best utilize the high bacteria loads in their food thrived and reproduced. Those dogs that could not tolerate the bacteria, died and did not reproduce. Through natural selection, the dog evolved efficient means of dealing with bacteria. Eating foods with a very high bacterial count, dogs became one of most successful mammal species in the world.

How do dogs handle such high bacterial count foods? We certainly do not have all the answers. There is a lot still unknown. We believe the primary defenses dogs evolved to protect themselves from dangerous bacteria are the length of time food spends in the stomach, and the short amount of time it spends in the intestines (gastric transit time); natural antibiotic secretions in the small intestines and in pancreatic fluids; and the large, diverse, and competitive natural viral, bacterial and fungal populations in the gut of the dog.

Gastric Transit Time in Dogs and Humans. The structure of the dog's digestive system (gut morphology) is somewhat different from that of humans. Compared to humans, the dog's gastrointestinal tract is relatively short[34,35,36] and the bolus (partially digested food) spends a much greater amount of time in the stomach.

The stomachs of dogs (and humans) make industrial strength hydrochloric acid that can dissolve iron. Dogs hold chewed food in their stomachs for 4 to 8[37,38] hours after ingestion. The low pH of the gastric juices provides a barrier to pathogens.[39] Only a little food at a time is released in to the intestine, which it passes through quickly.[40] This gives any bacteria that may live through the repeated acid baths little time to colonize and produce gastrointestinal distress.

In humans, on the other hand, the food may pass through the stomach into the intestines in as little as 30 to 60 minutes. The partially digested food may spend as long as 12 to 60 hours in the intestines before it is passed into the colon, and then defecated.[41] This means that "the intestines suffer prolonged exposure to whatever germs survive a minimal acid wash in the stomach."[42]

Cats will keep solid foods in their stomachs for about 12 hours.[43]

Time in Acid Bath of the Stomach	
Dogs	4–8 hours
Humans	30+ minutes

The transit time in the digestive system depends upon many factors, including meal size, viscosity (solid or liquid), particle size, density, caloric content, fat content, type of fats, water intake, outside temperature, amount and quality of exercise, stress level, health and age of the dog, and other factors. As in humans, there are wide individual differences.[44]

The data we've seen shows that cereal diets spend less time in the stomach than meat diets.[45] Cereal diets spend more time in the intestines, which may result in the same prolonged exposure experienced by humans eating a high-carbohydrate diet. Fiber, even finely ground, decreases transit time.[46] In our opinion, not enough hard data exists to draw firm conclusions on the difference in transit time between meat only, meat/grain mixtures and grain only diets.

Natural Antibiotic Secretions. Dogs have many defenses against potentially nasty bacteria. If bacteria survive the long acid-baths of the stomach, they must also withstand natural antibacterial secretions in the pancreas and the small intestines. The pancreatic fluids of dogs possess antibacterial properties.[47] Scientists have recently discovered that mammals secrete antibiotic molecules, called defensins, in the small intestines. Defensins are peptides which kill or inhibit the multiplication of invading bacteria. Each mammal species, based upon their evolutionary need, differs in the defensins made and which invading bacteria they kill or inhibit.[48]

The Intestines are a Competitive Environment. In humans, thousands of different species of microbes can live in the gut, although the average human has only several hundred different species, most likely based upon exposure to bacteria in the womb, during birth, and the first few months after birth.[49] The gut microbes outnumber all the cells in our bodies, perhaps by as much as a factor of 10.[50] In addition, our guts are teeming with 1,200 different viruses. Most of these viruses are phages, viruses that infect and kill bacteria.[51] We expect the same is true with the dog. This creates a highly competitive environment for invading bacteria. Existing bacteria don't give up their food and space without a fight. Some have developed highly effective weapons (often peptides) against other bacteria, fungi and other microbes. The microbes in the gut play a major protective role against new strains of bacteria entering from the outside.[52]

We hope the above has answered most people's questions as to why dogs can consume carrion and people cannot. We know many people and veterinarians have worried that the bacteria in raw foods may make them unsafe for dogs.

An open-minded examination of the evidence clearly shows that properly-prepared raw diets have a better safety record than dry or canned dog foods. First we'll look at why sterile foods like dry and canned dog foods can be dangerous. Then we'll look at the excellent safety record of proper raw diets. In Chapter 11 we'll document that dry dog foods inevitably contain potent toxins and allergens which may be one of the major contributing causes in canine cancer.

HOUSEFLIES AND THE DANGERS OF STERILE ENVIRONMENTS

"The destruction of spoilage microorganisms increases the storage life of the product. However, if this food is contaminated with pathogenic types of microorganisms, the natural competing flora is not present, and the food may become a health hazard." —George Banwart, *Basic Food Microbiology*, 1989.

Cooking creates a sterile environment, which is not natural and may be dangerous. For example, USDA data year after year shows that cooked products are recalled more often and are found to have harmful bacteria more often than raw products. From January 1997 to September 2000 there were 126 bacteria-related recalls. Of these, 41 were recalls of raw meat. 85 were recalls of cooked products.[53]

Let's examine why sterile environments can be dangerous, by looking at what can happen if a housefly lands on an open can of dog food or an open bag of dry dog food.

Canned dog foods are sterile environments until they are opened. Once opened, the food is an ideal breeding ground for bacteria. Since the food is sterile, the first species of bacteria that lands on the food can proliferate. Unlike raw foods, cooked foods contain no competing bacteria. The first species can, therefore, multiply very rapidly and become a danger to people, and perhaps even to dogs. The danger is a function of the number of bad bacteria and the virulence of that bacteria. One bad bacterium is not going to hurt anybody. Quadrillions and quadrillions of the same bacteria may be deadly.

Houseflies can easily infect food with bacteria and fungi. Flies have six legs, and experts have suggested that each footprint can carry 10,000 colonies of bacteria and thousands of fungal spores. Three recent studies showed that houseflies are capable of carrying and transmitting the *E. coli* O157:H7 strain, that is involved in human disease.[54] The housefly carrying the *E. coli* O157:H7 bacteria lands on an open sterile can of dog food. Every twenty minutes the population of these dangerous bacteria doubles since there are no competing bacteria to limit its growth. Soon there is a very dangerous situation. We tested this theory about exponential growth of bacteria at Food Products Laboratory, Portland, Oregon. A can of dog food was opened, inoculated with 1,000 CFU (Colony Forming Units) per gram of food, and allowed to incubate for two days at room temperatures. After 48 hours, the bacterial population increased by 15,000 times its original value. The conclusion from the food scientist: "(The canned dog food brand) was found to be an excellent growth medium for *E. coli* bacterium."[55]

Dry foods are not exempt from contamination by houseflies. Flies also carry spores of the *Aspergillus* mold. *Aspergillus flavus* mold produces Aflatoxin B1, the most potent naturally occurring carcinogenic substance known.[56] Iraqi officials admitted in 1995 to producing Aflatoxin to be used as a biological weapon.[57]

Spores from the *Aspergillus* mold are ubiquitous.[58] "It is a simple matter to fish an *Aspergillus* from the sky. Open a Petri dish anywhere outside the sterile air of an operating room for a few seconds, close the lid, and leave it for a day or so, and the plate will likely sprout... *Aspergillus*."[59] Some *Aspergillus* species survive the long trip from Africa to the Caribbean in dust clouds.[60]

The fly lands on the dry dog food, deposits a spore of *Aspergillus*. The *Aspergillus* mold prefers high carbohydrate food, and needs the trace minerals found in the dog food as well.[61] The dog food, initially very low in moisture, has gained moisture in the humid environment, allowing the mold to grow.[62] The *Aspergillus* mold is a storage fungus and can grow at moisture contents in equilibrium with relative humidities of 70 to 90% where no free water is available.)[63] The antimicrobials used by the manufacturer to delay mold growth are overwhelmed.[64] Since mold can grow in lower water activity (a measure of the amount of water available in food to support the growth of microbes) than bacteria,[65] there are few bacteria to compete with the mold. The food is served to the dog. Humans can't see small amounts of mold, and dogs can't taste low levels either.[66] Dogs are particularly vulnerable to the effects of aflatoxin.[67] Five years later, the dog dies from liver cancer.[68,69,70,71]

Back to our housefly. If the same housefly lands on a raw diet, the *E. coli* bacteria or mold spore it is carrying will not be able to proliferate. There is too much competition among the many species of bacteria for one species to dominate. Molds are more apt to be a health hazard in foods that do not support the growth of bacteria.[72,73]

THE SAFETY RECORD OF COMMERCIAL RAW DIETS
Commercial raw diets have been on the market for more than 20 years. Combined, our companies have probably fed more than 100,000

dogs without a single documented death due to bacterial problem. We know more than three fourths of the retailers who sell raw diets, have talked to hundreds of veterinarians, and met many thousands of consumers. Though some people worry about bacteria, and a small percentage of dogs have trouble with some foods, there have been no documented deaths.

The dry dog food industry does not have a good safety record. It is well documented that consumption of mycotoxin-contaminated dry dog foods has killed many dogs within hours of consumption. As we'll see in Chapter 11, Mycotoxins (the poisonous waste products of molds) are mostly long-term killers and may be the reason why one dog in three dies of cancer.

Now that we've seen that the dog's natural diet consisted of a variety of raw, often rotting, food, let's look at the nutrient content of the diet and compare it to dry dog food.

CHAPTER 6
The Macronutrient Content of the Dog's Natural Diet

From a macronutrient (protein, carbohydrate, water, and fat) point-of-view, the ancestral diet of dogs is almost the exact opposite of what most dogs are now being fed.

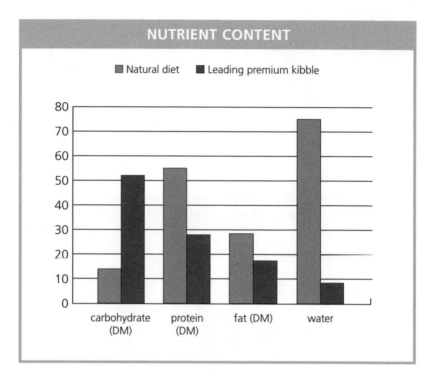

Dry Matter Basis. Food scientists analyze nutrient content of foods on a dry matter basis. Water, while a most important nutrient, provides no calories. Therefore, to analyze the protein, fat, and carbohydrate content of foods, we first eliminate the water and then look at what percentage of the food is protein, carbohydrate and fat. For example, let's analyze the protein in a typical raw diet and a typical dry dog food on a dry matter basis. Please see the formula for computing Dry Matter on the next page.

THE FORMULA

Protein (DM) = listed protein (%) divided by (1 minus water (%).

Most dry foods are in the 18 to 30% range for protein, and about 8% water (on an as fed basis). Let's choose the mid-point or 24% protein.

Protein (DM) equals 24% divided by (100% − 8%).
Protein (DM) = 0.24/(1 − 0.08) = 26%.

The dry matter protein of typical dry foods is about 26%. Most commercial raw diets have a minimum of 10% protein and 75% water.

Protein (DM) = 0.10/(1 − 0.75) = 40%.

LOW CARBOHYDRATE

The carbohydrate content of the natural diet of dogs is about 14%,[1] mostly from fruits and vegetables, with little if any from grains. (Prey animals, like rats, are usually less than 10% carbohydrate.)[2] Grains are a relatively recent food, even for humans. Grains were essentially absent from human nutrition until the invention of agriculture, which was only 10,000 years ago, and even then only in isolated areas.[3]

The carbohydrate content of dry foods ranges from 50 to 90%, mostly from grain. Grains are used because they provide inexpensive calories and are necessary to hold the dry foods together.

Grain Content of Foods Dogs Eat	
Natural Diet	Less Than 2%
Chicken	Less Than 2%
Dry Foods	45–90% Grain

Dogs do not normally eat grains. Dog food manufacturers spray a palatability enhancer, often called a digest, on the food after extrusion and drying to entice dogs to eat. With the digest, some manufacturers also spray on the vitamin/mineral mix, probiotics (live beneficial bacteria), and other heat fragile functional foods.

Digests are the results of chemical or enzymatic reactions of animal tissues, from meat, poultry, or fish. As such, they are considered "natural" flavors. Much of the research in dry pet foods is focused on getting dogs to eat the food. In *Petfood Industry*, a magazine for people producing pet foods, the back cover and the inside front cover are usually advertisements from companies producing palatability enhancers.

Dogs do not need carbohydrates in their diet at all, as long as they eat a high protein diet that meets the energy requirements of the dog. All three major textbooks used in veterinary schools in the US agree.

Do Dogs Need Carbohydrates?

Canine and Feline Nutrition (co-authored by two scientists from Iams®): "The fact that dogs and cats do not require carbohydrate is immaterial because the nutrient content of most commercial foods include (carbohydrates)."[4]

Small Animal Clinical Nutrition III, written by the founder of Science Diet® (Mark Morris Sr.) and his son (Mark Morris Jr.): "Some question exists regarding the need of dogs and cats for dietary carbohydrate. From a practical sense, the answer to this question is of little importance because there are carbohydrates in most food ingredients used in commercially prepared dog foods.[5]

The Waltham Book of Companion Animal Nutrition: "There is no known minimum dietary requirement for carbohydrate...."[6]

High carbohydrate diets are, in our opinions, not healthy for dogs. Scientists are now learning that high grain-supplied carbohydrate diets are not healthy for people either. Humans, though, are better equipped to digest grain than dogs are. The saliva of humans contains an enzyme (alpha-amylase) which starts digestion when food is chewed. We believe, but have seen conflicting data, that the dog's saliva does not naturally contain this enzyme; consequently the digestion of starch takes place only in the small intestine.[7]

Is Carbohydrate a Dirty Word? You won't find carbohydrate listed on your dog food bag. Foods are composed primarily of water, carbohydrate, fat and protein. In the guaranteed analysis, required on every dog food or treat sold in the U.S., you'll find water, protein, fat, and fiber. The word "carbohydrate" is almost never mentioned.

Pet foods are regulated on a state-by-state basis by members of the Association of American Feed Control Officials (AAFCO). Manufacturers must send labels (and checks!) for all the pet foods they sell to the association member in each state, who then reviews the label and issues a license to allow sale of that product in the state. Most state members follow the model regulations as designated by AAFCO. If a label does not follow AAFCO regulations, the state regulator may decide not to license the product. If the product is sold without a license, the regulator can go into a store and remove the product. Not a good thing to happen to a pet food manufacturer. Therefore almost all pet food companies play by AAFCO's rules (some help make them).

AAFCO guidelines, as published in the Official Publication of the Association of American Feed Control Officials, discourage the use of the word "carbohydrate" anywhere on a pet food label. Here are the exact words:

> "... carbohydrate guarantees are no longer considered as necessary or meaningful for purchaser information, therefore, their future use is discouraged. (Combination of four resolutions adopted prior to 1923, amended 1963)."[8]

During the summer 2004 AAFCO meeting, AAFCO will address the issue of listing carbohydrate on the label. They can rescind the policy of discouraging the listing of carbohydrate, or they may reinforce it, or do nothing. Chances are, no decision will be made. The reader may learn about AAFCO at www.aafco.org.

Pet food literature is not regulated by AAFCO, but one can still rarely find "carbohydrate" mentioned, whether in technical manuals for veterinarians or dog guardians. For example, in the publication for veterinarians, *Applied Clinical Nutrition of the Dog and Cat, A Guide to Waltham® Veterinary Diets* the word "carbohydrate" is not even mentioned in the 44 page technical discussion of their Veterinary Canine Calorie Control diet and Canine Restricted Protein diets. Waltham lists protein, fat, ash, crude fiber content and 12 minerals, 11 vitamins, 11 amino acids, but not carbohydrates. "Only 13% of the calories in Waltham® Veterinary Diet Canine Low Protein (dry) are derived from protein, compared with 25 to 30% in a typical dry dog food."[9] They, of course, don't mention that they increased the carbohydrate content of the food.

Calculating Carbohydrates. To calculate the carbohydrate content of a dry food, one must estimate the ash or mineral content of the food.

THE FORMULA

100% –% water –% protein –% fat –% ash = % carbohydrate (on an as fed basis).

Remember fat and protein listed as minimums, water as maximum. Typical ash content of high quality dry pet foods is generally between 5 and 8%.[10]

For example, a typical "maintenance" dog food is 21% protein (min), 11% fat (min), and 10% moisture (max). Using 7% as the ash content of the food, the approximate carbohydrate content of the food is 100 –21 –11 –10 –7, which equals 51%, on an as fed basis (57% on a dry matter basis.)

Carbohydrates and Obesity. At least half the dogs we meet are over-weight. Just as with people, an increasing number of dogs are being diagnosed with diabetes.[11] We think there are two reasons: high carbohydrate diets and lack of exercise. Several recent studies with people show that lower carbohydrate diets like those recommended by Atkins, the Eades, Mercola, and Sears are more effective than traditional diet plans for losing weight.[12] Humans, unlike dogs, have some dietary need for carbohydrates. Our experience shows that obese dogs usually lose weight when converted from high carbohydrate dry dog foods to proper raw diets. See the "Keep Your Dog Lean" section of Chapter 16 for more information.

HIGH QUALITY AND QUANTITY PROTEIN

"Diets that are rich in complex carbohydrates will also favor the development of certain tapeworms and intestinal protozoa, such as amoebe, whereas a high-protein diet will work against the growth of such parasites."[13]

The natural diet of the dog is high in protein. Almost every-thing the dog ate in the wild was high in protein—high quality animal protein. We calculate from the information in *Diet of Feral Carnivores* that the typical diet of a dog consisted of 56% protein (on a dry matter, DM, basis).

The protein content of most dry foods ranges from 20% to 30% on a dry matter basis. Much of this protein is low-quality protein from grain. In a typical "premium" lamb and rice product, for example, 26% is lamb, and 63% is grain.

Dogs Need Meat, Not Grain. While some dogs live quite well on high carbohydrate diets, many do not. Our goal with this book is to increase the odds that all our dogs will live long healthy lives. Dogs need a meat-based diet, preferably raw, to do this. The pet food industry is continually learning more about the need for meat and high quality protein. This is especially true for cats. A 2002 article in the *Journal of the American Veterinary Medical Association* concluded: "although cats have adjusted to most manufactured diets, the limitations of substituting animal-origin nutrients with plant-origin nutrients in foods formulated for cats are being increasingly realized."[14] We'll discuss just two examples with dogs: taurine and L-carnitine.

Lack of taurine in commercial cat foods caused much suffering for many years. Taurine, a sulfur-containing amino acid present in raw animal muscle tissue, is essential for cats. Cats, unlike most dogs and people, cannot make their own taurine: It must be supplied by the diet. Much of the taurine in meat is lost during cooking, and plant products contain only minute amounts of taurine.[15] In the first few decades of the commercial pet food industry, before the industry learned about taurine deficiency (1987) and added taurine to cat foods, many cats that ate commercial cat food and did not eat fresh mice or birds suffered from taurine deficiency. Some of the health problems resulting from lack of taurine included central retinal degeneration (an eye problem), dilated cardiomyopathy (a heart problem), reproductive failure and impaired fetal development.[16] Even now, the pet food industry nutrient standards (the AAFCO nutrient profiles) may underestimate the amount of taurine needed by cats.[17]

We are now learning that the lack of taurine in the diet may be creating heart problems with some dogs fed lamb meal and rice or tofu-based diets. Scientists at The University of California, Davis, world leaders in understanding feline nutrition (and therefore experts in taurine) report: "Diet-related taurine deficiencies and associated dilated cardiomyopathies have been reported in large breed dogs. The present investigators have recently reported taurine deficiency (52%) and cardiac insufficiency (10%) among a group of 21 privately-owned Newfoundland dogs."[18] It's not just large breeds that may have taurine-deficiency problems on lamb and rice diets. The American Cocker Spaniel is well-known to have taurine and carnitine-responsive dilated cardiomyopathy.[19] With Steve's Charlee Bear Dogs, three dogs have died of heart problems—all were eating a major national brand lamb and rice diet.

Several dog food manufacturers are now adding taurine to their lamb and rice diets to help correct this issue.

"L-carnitine: Evidence indicates it may accelerate weight loss and increase lean body mass," is the title of an article by Tim Phillips, DVM, editor of *Petfood Industry*, in the May, 2002 issue. He continues: "Carnitine deficiency is a proven cause of heart disease in dogs.... Most pet foods are relatively low in L-carnitine due to the types of ingredients used. Even though L-carnitine is present in both plant and animal ingredients, ingredient processing removes significant amounts of it. Wild-type diets for dogs and cats (meat or whole carcass) provide significantly more L-carnitine than commercial pet foods."[20]

Controlled studies with sled dogs show that those dogs fed diets high in fat and protein and very low in carbohydrate outperform those fed moderate or high carbohydrate diets.[21]

Protein Content (DM) of Foods Dogs Eat	
Rabbit	80%
Natural Diet	56%
Commercial Raw Diets	45+%
Dry Foods	20–30%

Not All Proteins Are The Same. Proteins are very large molecules that consist of chains of hundreds of much smaller sub-units called amino acids. There are 22 different types of amino acids.[22] Animals need dietary protein to provide the specific amino acids that their tissues cannot synthesize. **Essential amino acids** are those that cannot be made by the body in sufficient quantities and must be supplied in the food. High quality proteins, like eggs and most meats, consist of a full range of the essential amino acids. Low quality proteins, like the protein in most grains, consist of only some of the essential amino acids.

Animal proteins generally have a more balanced amino acid profile and better digestibility than plant proteins.[23] Protein quality is often measured in biologic value—the percentage of the protein that is absorbed and retained, not excreted. The higher the biologic value, the better the quality of the protein. Meats have much higher biologic values than grains. For example, the biologic value of beef is 78%, corn is 45%.[24]

What a radical change! In just 50 years the dog's diet changed from high quality, high quantity protein, to low quality, low quantity protein.

HIGH WATER CONTENT

"During the past 30 years there has been a 1,500% increase in the incidence of bloat, and this has coincided with the increased feeding of dry dog foods."[25]

Most of the natural foods dogs ate contained a high water content. Water is essential for digestion. The dog's digestive system evolved with some, if not most, of the water necessary for digestion coming from the food the dog ate. Now, with dry food, little of the water comes from the food, and the dog's digestive system must produce the water. This is a dramatic and rapid (by evolutionary standards) change in what the dog's digestive system must do.

Dogs that eat proper raw diets—about 75% water—drink much less water than those that eat dry dog food. Could the lack of water in dry dog food be a contributing factor in bloat? Dr. Jerold

Bell, in The Healthy Dog column for the April 2003 *AKC* (American Kennel Club) *Gazette* stated: "During the past 30 years, there has been a 1,500% increase in the incidence of bloat, and this has coincided with the increased feeding of dry dog foods."[26]

Many studies have indicated that feeding a high moisture diet may reduce the risk of calcium oxalate stone disease.[27]

Water Content of Foods Dogs Eat	
Chickens	70%
Apples	90%
Grass	70%
Beef Bone	45%
Commercial Raw Diets	75%
Dry Foods	8%

HIGH QUALITY FATS

There is some debate about the amount of fat in the ancestral diet. Some people believe that the natural diet of dogs was low in fat, because wild animals would have been lean. True, wild animals had less fat than today's feed animals. Fat animals didn't survive in the wild. But all wild animals had parts that were fatty, and dogs tended to eat those parts. For example, typical beef bones (the marrow is mostly fat) are 50 to 60% fat on a dry matter (DM) basis.[28] 70% of the calories in beef brains are from fat[29] and the nerve fibers throughout the central nervous system are surrounded by a fatty layer.[30] Fish guts can be 20% fat or more, and the guts of animals, not eaten by humans and tossed to the dogs, also have high fat contents. Brains and spinal cords, common foods for dogs, are high in fat. Modern rats are 55% protein, 38.1% fat, 9.1% carbohydrate.[31]

Dr. Donald Strombeck, Professor Emeritus, University California,

Davis, School of Veterinary Medicine thinks that the natural diet of carnivores was rich in fat. He also states that "increasing a pet food's fat content increases its cost; therefore, most commercial pet foods are low-fat."[32] Our calculations and studies suggest that the ancestral diet of dogs was about 25 to 30% fat (DM); it provided equal amount of calories from fat and protein. Fat has 9 kilocalories per gram, protein and carbohydrate kilocalories per gram for human-edible foods. For "pet food quality," since it is less digestible, fat is calculated at 8.5 kcal/g, protein and carbohydrate at 3.5 kcal/g.

The amount of fat in the diet is important, but the quality of fat may be just as important. The dog's evolutionary diet contained a higher percentage of omega-3 fatty acids and fewer saturated fats than today's domesticated plants and animals normally provide.[33] The benefits of omega-3 fatty acids for both humans and dogs are well documented. They include protection against heart disease, allergies, diabetes, progressive retinal atrophy (an eye problem), and brain development in the womb.[34] Dr. John Bauer, one of the leading veterinary nutritionists in the country, wrote: "Omega-3 fatty acids are critically important in pet neuromuscular development, skin health, and coat quality."[35]

Pet food regulators, through the Association of American Feed Control Officials (AAFCO) have not yet established minimum requirements for omega-3 fatty acids in dog foods. Hence most dry and wet dog foods do not contain these important, in our opinions, essential fatty acids. This will change in the near future. The National Research Council's Subcommittee on Dog and Cat Nutrition has released a pre-publication version of the report *Nutrient Requirements of Dogs and Cats*. Omega-3 fatty acids are the only "new" nutrients for which specific requirements have been set by this report. The pet food industry, through the Pet Food Institute, is challenging many of the findings in this report, including the new concept (for the NRC pet food committee) of safe upper limits.[36] AAFCO will base its future recommendations on the final version of this report. We expect that in a few years, omega-3 fatty acids will be required in all dog foods.

A RADICAL CHANGE IN A VERY SHORT TIME

In a matter of 50 to 100 years, the diets of dogs have changed radically, from low carbohydrate, high protein, high-quality fat and high water content diets to high carbohydrate, low protein, low-quality fat, and low water content diets.

The macronutrients are not the entire story. As we'll see, the change in the micronutrient content of dog's diets has been just as radical.

CHAPTER 7

The Micronutrient Content of the Dog's Natural Diet

The Dog's Natural Diet Provides
Vitamins and minerals in natural forms Full range of antioxidants, minerals and other nutrients Thousands of different types of enzymes

Dogs, like people, need to eat real, natural, foods, not just processed food with added vitamin/mineral pills. Micronutrients are the vitamins, minerals, antioxidants, enzymes, and other nutrients that are found in food. Macronutrients are protein, carbohydrate (including fiber), fat, and water.

In this chapter, we're going to look at the difference between the full range of natural micronutrients provided by the ancestral diets of dogs and the limited number of human-synthesized micronutrients provided in the dogs' modern diet. First, we'll show that there is a significant nutritional difference between natural forms of micronutrients and human-synthesized forms. We will then show that the dogs' natural diet contained a full range—thousands—of different micronutrients, compared to the limited number in dry and canned foods, and third, we'll examine the value of enzymes, available in the natural diet but not in most dry and canned pet foods.

First let's look at the ingredients in a top-selling premium dry dog food and compare it to the ingredients in a premium commercial raw diet that is based upon the ancestral diet of dogs.

Top Selling Premium Dry Dog Food

Chicken, corn meal, ground grain sorghum, ground wheat, chicken by-product meal, brewers rice, soybean meal, animal fat (preserved with mixed tocopherols and citric acid), chicken liver flavor, vegetable oil, dried egg product, flaxseed, preserved with mixed tocopherols and citric acid, minerals (salt, calcium carbonate, potassium chloride, dicalcium phosphate, ferrous sulfate, zinc oxide, copper sulfate, manganous oxide, calcium iodate, sodium selenite), rosemary extract, beta-carotene, vitamins (choline chloride, vitamin A supplement, vitamin D3 supplement, vitamin E supplement, L-ascorbyl-2-polyphosphate (a source of vitamin C), niacin, thiamine mononitrate, calcium pantothenate, pyridoxine hydro-chloride, riboflavin, folic acid, biotin, vitamin B12 supplement).

Premium Commercial Raw Diet

Chicken (muscle meat, bones, liver, heart) carrots, broccoli, squash, yams, parsnips, sui choi, spinach, kale, parsley, garlic, olive oil, kelp. (Amoré Pet Foods, Richmond, BC Canada)

VITAMINS AND MINERALS IN NATURAL FORM

Eat your vegetables and you consume natural forms of micronutrients. Take a vitamin/mineral pill and you consume human-synthesized forms. There is a world of difference.

Dozens of books and hundreds of published, peer-reviewed studies, including the most recent Institute of Medicine reports, show that people and laboratory animals that eat fresh vegetables and fruits are healthier and have lower incidences of cancer, stroke and heart disease than those whose intake of micronutrients is primarily from human-made forms.

We believe this is true with dogs as well. Yet most dogs now get almost all their vitamins and minerals in synthetic, human-made, forms.

To document the importance of consuming micronutrients from natural sources, we'll review a few of the recent studies on the need for people and laboratory animals to eat whole foods. Then, as an example, we will take a closer look at one micronutrient, selenium, to show why dogs, like people, need to eat real foods.

Vitamins and Essential Nutrients. Vitamins are micronutrients that are essential for life and must be supplied by the diet. Without vitamins, dogs cannot be healthy. Many vitamins (including C, A and E) are antioxidants. Vitamins for dogs and vitamins for people differ. For example, vitamin C is essential for humans (without vitamin C, humans get scurvy). Dogs, on the other hand, make their own vitamin C and therefore it is not considered essential for dogs.[1] Choline is considered essential for dogs, but not for people.

Some minerals are also essential for health, sometimes in very minute quantities (these are called trace minerals). The essential fatty acids (EFAs) are those specific fats which must be supplied by the diet. Nutrition is a young, dynamic science. The word vitamin was just coined in 1912. In 1958, free radicals were discovered. Today, when we think of disease-fighting nutrients, we don't just examine vitamins. We study the phytochemicals, flavonoids and antioxidants, with new micronutrients being discovered weekly. For example, lipoic acid is a powerful antioxidant that some prominent researchers believe should be given vitamin status in humans.[2] Lipoic acid is the only known antioxidant that is both water and fat soluble. It is produced by animals and humans, but in minuscule quantities, disqualifying it from gaining vitamin status.

As nutritionists learn about micronutrients, nutrient recommendations change. As previously mentioned, the National Research Council of the National Academy of Sciences released its 2003 prepublication report *Nutrient Requirements of Dogs and Cats*. This is the first update on nutrient recommendations for dogs and cats since 1986. In this report, omega-3 fatty acids are, for the first time, considered essential fatty acids. In the next NRC update, probably in year 2015–2020, we expect that lipoic acid, L-carnitine and taurine will be considered essential nutrients for dogs.

Every week we read of new studies showing that nutrients in whole foods protect humans and laboratory animals from cancer and cardiovascular problems, while, in many cases, the pill forms of the same nutrients have proved to be no more effective than placebos.[3] The more research that is done on supplements, the less effective they turn out to be. Below are some conclusions from recent studies and prominent researchers.

> "The variety of nutrients with potential cancer preventative properties, as well as the undiscovered cancer preventative constituents of foods, argues against a supplement-only approach to enhancing health and cancer prevention."[4]

"Combinations of nutrients found in foods have greater protective effects than each nutrient taken alone."[5]

"Antioxidant vitamins… did not produce any significant reductions in the 5-year mortality from, or incidence of, any type of vascular disease, cancer, or other major outcome."[6]

"Consumption of tomato powder but not lycopene inhibited prostate carcinogenisis, suggesting that tomato products contain compounds in addition to lycopene that modify prostate carcinogenisis."[7]

"Folate used in food fortification is not a natural coenzyme; we do not know the long term biological effects of exposure to unmodified synthetic folate."[8]

"Dietary supplementation, long presumed to be purely beneficial, may have unintended deleterious influences…" including the possibility that excess folic acid may play a role in disorders like obesity or autism.[9]

Supplements Are Not The Same As Food. Supplements containing vitamins A, C and E, and beta-carotene "have failed to demonstrate a consistent or significant effect of any single vitamin or combination of vitamins" in reduction of cancer, heart disease and deaths from both. "The USPSTF (US Preventive Services Task Force) recommends against the use of beta-carotene supplements, either alone or in combination, for the prevention of cancer or cardiovascular disease. **This is a grade D recommendation.**" Grade D means that the USPSTF found at least fair evidence that beta-carotene is ineffective or that its harm outweighs its benefits.[10]

The Institute of Medicine of the National Academies, in a 2004 report on potassium states that food sources of potassium (vegetables and fruits) are superior to supplements. The report does not even consider potassium chloride to a viable form of potassium.[11] Yet almost all dry dog foods use potassium chloride, not vegetables and fruits, as the source of potassium.

Eating fresh vegetables and fruits is especially important when the dog is pregnant because of the demands of the fetuses. Long-term studies with humans in poor countries show that eating green vegetables in order to obtain micronutrients boosted the birth-weights of the babies (an important factor in the health of the adult), while human-synthesized, pure compound supplements had no effect on birth-weight when given to pregnant women.[12]

We believe one of the reasons proper raw diets with vegetables and fruits often correct many different health problems with dogs is that the dog (and the human) evolved to use natural forms of vitamins, minerals and other micronutrients, and may not be able to fully use human-made forms. As an example, let's take a closer look at the forms of selenium in real foods as compared to the form used in most dog foods and make some guesses as to one of the potential causes of Canine Hip Dysplasia.

Sodium Selenite Does Not Equal Selenomethionine. Selenium is an essential trace mineral of fundamental importance to human and canine health. It is receiving considerable attention for its possible role as an effective naturally occurring anti-carcinogenic agent. Recently, the American Association for Cancer Research reported that high selenium consumption may protect humans from bladder cancer.[13]

Dogs evolved consuming two organic forms of selenium: selenomethionine (an essential amino acid found primarily in plants) and selenocysteine (an amino acid found mostly in organ meats). Most dry and canned dog foods today use an inorganic type of selenium, sodium selenite or sodium selenate. These forms of selenium are considered toxic by the National Toxicology Program of the US Department of Health and Human Services.[14]

The body reacts differently to the selenium in food as compared to food supplemented with sodium selenite. A 2003 study in *The Journal of Nutrition* stated that "the absorption, distribution, and excretion of seleniuim in food were... distinctly different from sodium selenite."[15] Natural forms of selenium are superior to human synthesized forms. Dr. John W Finley, supervisor of the Trace Element Absorption and Bioavailability Laboratory and the Grand Forks Human Nutrition Research Center, and one of the leading researchers on selenium stated:

> "Something in the whole foods must boost selenium's anticancer property [and these] results are further evidence that broccoli may be an especially good source of selenium, and nutrition professionals may be wise to take this information into account when giving nutritional advice."[16]

Insufficient selenium intake can cause serious health problems, including Kashin-Beck disease which is characterized by the degeneration of the articular cartilage between joints.[17] We've read unpublished, yet well researched, reports linking selenium deficiency with hip dysplasia.[18] There is a wealth of data about farm animals which shows organic forms of selenium (selenomethionine) outperform sodium selenite. One of the reasons for this is that natural forms of selenium can be stored in the body, while selenite cannot.[19] Perhaps some dogs are not able to sufficiently use the inorganic forms of selenium found in most dry dog foods. Therefore if a bitch were unable to fully utilize sodium selenite, her puppies would be more likely to have joint problems (see discussion on genes, womb effect and environment in the appendix). Pottenger's classic study with cats shows that problems due to nutrient deficiency get worse with each generation.[20]

Is the source of the selenium used in most dry dog foods one of the reasons many dogs, purebred and mixed-breed, have hip problems? It may be one of the nutritional causes. The inorganic forms of copper, zinc, or iron that are used in dog foods may also be factors. Or perhaps it's a micronutrient that we just don't know about yet.

FULL RANGE OF MICRONUTRIENTS

The dog's natural diet contained thousands of different types of antioxidants, a full range of minerals, and probably thousands of different types of enzymes. The modern dry dog food diet contains just a few types of antioxidants, most minerals but not all that may be required, and no enzymes.

Complete Families of Antioxidants. Antioxidants are a group of compounds that are produced by the body and occur naturally in many foods. Plants produce certain types of antioxidants (polyphenolics) as a defense against insects and other pests. Study after study with humans and laboratory animals show that antioxidants help prevent aging and other diseases.[21] Dr. Lester Packer, Director of the Packer Lab at the University of California, Berkeley, and one of the leading researchers on antioxidants, shows that antioxidants "work together in the body to maintain our health and vigor.... There is overwhelming scientific evidence demonstrating that those of us who eat a diet rich in antioxidants... will live longer, healthier lives."[22]

Vitamin C, A and E are three of the better known antioxidants. In natural foods, there are thousands of natural antioxidants. There are more than 4,000 flavonoids, a class of antioxidants found in fruits and vegetables.[23] Vitamin A is a generic term for a large number of related compounds, not just a single chemical. There are at least 15 different major compounds in the Vitamin A group.[24,25] Most dry dog food manufacturers add just one of the compounds.

The point is, humans need to consume antioxidants in food, not vitamin pills. We need to eat cantaloupe, not take a beta-carotene supplement. There are hundreds of different carotenoids in cantaloupe. Beta-carotene is just one of them. Indeed, recent studies show that beta-carotene pills may be dangerous. "Beta-carotene led to a small but significant increase in all-cause death, and a small increase in cardiovascular death. The researchers find the beta-carotene results especially concerning since the doses that produced this effect were within the range commonly used in over-the-counter preparations." [26] We see no reason to think that synthetic or isolated vitamins are any better for dogs and cats than they are for humans.

Let's examine apples and see why an apple is much superior to a vitamin pill. The study "Antioxidant Activity in Fresh Apples" published in *Nature*, concluded that "almost all of the antioxidant activity in apples must be due to phytochemicals… (phenolic acids and flavonoids), as these are natural antioxidants." [27]

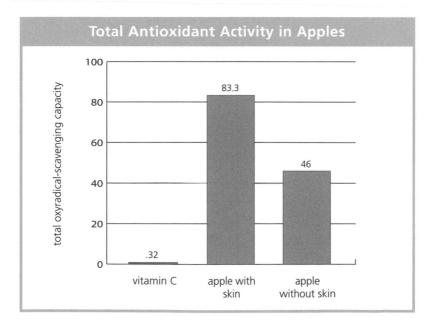

Vitamin C provides little (0.4%) of the antioxidant activity of apples. Quercetin is just one of the many antioxidant compounds in apples that scientists believe helps prevent cancer. One can't just take a quercetin pill either. Like many pure compounds, quercetin in high doses shows evidence of carcinogenic activity.[28] Much of the antioxidant activity of apples is provided by unknown micronutrients.

Vitamin C is not the only micronutrient in an orange, either. In addition to vitamin C, oranges provide potassium, calcium, phosphorous, selenium, folate, vitamins A and E and other micronutrients.

A Complete Range of Trace Minerals. Since the dog evolved eating the leftovers and waste products of humans, eating somewhat the same foods as humans, we expect their needs for minerals to be similar. Minerals are elements: They cannot be produced within the body, they must be consumed. Probably because of lack of research, the AAFCO's nutrient guidelines require fewer minerals than U.S. government guidelines for human nutrition require. Below is a list of the minerals considered essential for humans (*Dietary Reference Intakes, The National Academies, 2001. www.nap.edu.) and for dogs (AAFCO Dog Food Nutrient Profiles, 2003. www.aafco.org.).

Mineral	Essential, humans	Essential, dogs
Calcium	e	e
Phosphorus	e	e
Magnesium	e	e
Sodium	e	e
Potassium	e	e
Chloride	e	e
Iron	e	e
Copper	e	e
Zinc	e	e
Manganese	e	e
Selenium	e	e
Iodine	e	e
Boron	e	
Chromium	e	
Molybdenum	e	
Silicon	e	
Nickel	e	
Vanadium	e	

Boron and chromium are trace minerals (essential in very small amounts—a few milligrams per day) which are just now being recognized as important for optimal long-term health in human nutrition. These nutrients are not yet considered essential by the pet food regulators and therefore may be absent in many processed pet foods. Boron may be essential for brain and psychological function[29] and may play an essential role in bone metabolism.[30] The Committee on Animal Nutrition, National Research Council, concluded: "sufficient evidence is available which, when taken together with observations made with humans, indicates that chromium may be an essential nutrient for animals."[31] Boron is obtained from a diet rich in fruits, vegetables, nuts and legumes. Chromium is obtained from liver, fish, meat and certain whole grains. Fluoride, molybdenum, cobalt, tin, nickel, vanadium, and silicon are other essential trace minerals for humans, but not yet considered essential for dogs. Are these minerals essential to sustain the dog's life? No. Are they essential for optimum health? Probably. People and dogs that eat a variety of real foods consume these micronutrients. Those that get their trace minerals from supplements provided in commercial dog food probably do not consume these minerals.

Many of the micronutrients that we're discussing in this book were unknown to leading nutrition researchers just 20 years ago. Human nutritional scientists are learning rapidly about the value of certain nutrients in whole foods. For example, in April 2003 Japanese scientists discovered a new substance, pyrroloquinoline quinine, that they considered to be a vitamin (essential nutrient) for rats and, they speculated, probably for humans as well. Mice deprived of PQQ suffer reduced fertility and roughened fur. PQQ is naturally found in parsley, green tea and green peppers.[32] Perhaps, in a few decades, PQQ will be considered a vitamin for dogs and added to dry dog foods.

Real foods contain micronutrients about which scientists know little or nothing, some of which we may find to be of importance. We're finding over and over again that what we left out did turn out to be important. There is no question; humans need real food, with a full range of antioxidants and minerals to, be at their best. We are certain this is true with dogs as well.

Thousands of Different Types of Enzymes. Raw foods, especially meats, contain thousands of different types of enzymes. Enzymes are the body's workers and are essential for all of life's operations. All live cells, plant and animal, contain enzymes. "The biological processes that occur within all living organisms are chemical reactions, and most are regulated by enzymes. Without enzymes, many of these reactions would not take place at a perceptible rate. Enzymes catalyze [help a chemical reaction to take place without being itself consumed in the reaction] all aspects of cell metabolism. This includes the digestion of food, in which large nutrient molecules (such as proteins, carbohydrates, and fats) are broken down into smaller molecules."[33]

We require enzymes to digest food. Some enzymes occur naturally in food; digestive enzymes are made by the body. Different enzymes help digest different types of food. Proteases break down proteins, lipases fats, and amylases work on carbohydrates. (Those who are lactose intolerant don't produce enough of the enzyme lactase, which digests lactose).

Cooked foods have no enzymes. When food is cooked above 110°F. the enzymes' intramolecular bonds are overcome by thermal fluctuations and break. This changes its overall shape and results in a denatured or "dead" enzyme. Therefore there are no enzymes in dry or canned dog foods. When a dog eats cooked foods, the dog's pancreas, stomach and small intestine must make all enzymes necessary for digestion. This may put a long-term strain on these organs.[34] The enzymes in raw foods help with digestion, reducing the load on the dog's digestive organs.

The nutritional value of enzymes in dogs' diets has been shown in many published studies in peer-reviewed scientific journals. We have also personally heard, from dog guardians, many success stories about the improvement in their dogs' health with the addition of enzymes to the diet.

Dr. Randy Wysong in his book *Lipid Digestion* documents eight studies showing that enzymes are able to survive the rigors of digestion.[35] Dr. Howell, a noted researcher who has studied enzymes for 50 years, notes that animal meats "are amply provided with cathepsin." (Cathepsin is a type of enzyme called a protease that is present in most animal organ meats). When dogs eat meat, their stomachs secrete cathepsin to digest the meat. Dr. Howell notes that gastric secreted cathepsin and food cathepsin operate in similar acid solutions, pH 3 to 4. He states "the cathepsin within the meat itself lightens the burden of digestion for its counterpart in the warm confines of the stomach."[36] Dr. Lowell Ackerman, using blood sample analysis, found that an enzyme supplement, Prozyme™, enhances the bioavailability (the body's ability to use) zinc, selenium and linoleic acid.[37]

Some traditional pet food scientists claim that enzymes are all deactivated—made unusable—by the stomach acids. We think for the most part this is not true. Enzymes the dog consumes that are meant to work in the stomach, like cathepsin, are meant to work in a highly acidic environment. Consuming these enzymes will reduce the load of the dog's digestive system. When the dog consumes enzymes that help digest food in the small intestine, these enzymes will, most likely, be deactivated in the acid baths of the stomach. These enzymes will have at least some effect in the stomach before they encounter the acid gastric juices. As frozen foods defrost, the enzymes begin the work, starting to digest the meat and fat and carbohydrate. Even if these enzymes do not survive the stomach acid baths, they have already helped in digestion.[38]

As we grow older, the body's ability to produce enzymes decreases.[39] This is probably one of the reasons we see such outstanding results when we convert dogs from an enzyme-depleted dry dog food diet to an enzyme-rich raw diet.

PART TWO
Conclusion

In this part of the book we've examined the dog's ancestral diet. For 99.997% or more of the history of dogs they ate a variety of raw, real foods teeming with germs. The dog's gut morphology allows the dog to thrive on bacteria-laden foods that have the potential to kill humans. The foods the dog ate were high in protein, fat, and water, and low in carbohydrate. These foods also contained thousands of cancer-fighting antioxidants and enzymes in their natural form and balance.

Today's canine diet is almost exactly the opposite. Most dogs get almost no dietary variety (if people follow the advice of a leading dog food company). The food they eat is low in protein and water and high in carbohydrate. Dogs get most of their vitamins and minerals in human-made forms, with no proven cancer-fighting agents, and no longer consume the thousands of antioxidants and other micronutrients that their natural diet contained.

This radical change in the macro- and micronutrient contents of the diet is one of the reasons we see many health problems with both purebred and mixed-breed dogs. But it's only half the story. Dogs have always eaten less than human-edible foods. Now, though, less than human-edible meats may contain potent human-made toxins, and less than human-edible grains inevitably contain potent poisons, called mycotoxins, which cause cancer. Steve thinks it was the mycotoxins in dry dog food that killed Zach.

What is natural or "holistic" about dry dog food?

Not the protein
Not the carbohydrate
Not the fat
Not the micronutrients

PART THREE
Carcinogens and Allergens in Pet Foods

"Dietary carcinogens are believed to play a greater role in causing cancer than was previously thought. Most of the specific carcinogens have not yet been characterized. Aflatoxins, generated by molds in grain, are one example...."[1]

Dogs evolved eating the waste products of human villages: ancient versions of "less than human-edible foods." They ate almost anything with calories that was left over: scraps, fish heads and all sorts of foods with heavy bacterial loads. Things that humans didn't want to eat back in primitive days must have been gross indeed! Gross, but usually not laden with the carcinogens (substances that have been shown to cause cancer) that many of today's dry dog foods contain.

Potent toxins (poisons) and allergens are unavoidable in dry dog foods, from both the high temperature cooking and the less than human edible ingredients used in most commercial dog foods. We believe these toxins are a major contributing factor to the high cancer rate in dogs. The chances are that the less expensive the food, the lower the quality of ingredients, the more toxins the food contains.

First, we will look at typical dry dog food recipes, and the costs of the ingredients used.

CHAPTER 8
Recipes and Costs

Dry dog foods are popular because they are inexpensive. They are inexpensive because dry dog foods have low production costs (some extruders can produce up to 50,000 pounds of dog food per hour), and most brands use inexpensive ingredients.

Before we explore the toxins in the dry foods, let's take a close look at what is in dry dog food. The next two tables show the recipes and cost of ingredients for a grocery store brand food and a premium brand dry food.

Grocery Store Brand Dry Dog Food		
Overall Ingredient Cost, Ten Cents Per Pound		
Ingredient	*% in Recipe*	*Cost/lb.*
CORN	57 %	5.2¢
SOYBEAN MEAL	21%	9.5¢
MEAT & BONE MEAL	11%	10¢
BEEF TALLOW	5 %	13¢
WATER	2.5%	0
PRESERVATIVE MIX	1.25%	$1.70
SALT	0.5%	3.4¢
CARMEL COLOR	0.40%	60¢
CANOLA OIL	0.3%	25¢
CHOLINE CHLORIDE	0.1%	50¢
MINERAL MIX	0.05%	35¢
VITAMIN MIX	0.05%	$1.95
COLOR–RED	0.002%	$5.50
POTASSIUM SORBATE	0.001%	$1.75

"Premium" Dry Dog Food

Overall Ingredient Cost Twenty Cents Per Pound (includes 8% shrinkage—
100 pounds ingredients equal 92 pounds of product)

Ingredient	*% in recipe*	*Cost/lb.*
CHICKEN MEAL	30%	$0.26
CRACKED BARLEY	27%	$0.13
BREWERS RICE	26%	$0.09
POULTRY FAT	10%	$0.23
DIGEST	3%	$0.47
TOMATO POMACE	2%	$0.09
POTASSIUM CHLORIDE	0.5%	$0.10
SALT	0.25%	$0.03
VITAMIN MIX	0.10%	$4.50
MINERAL MIX	0.10%	$0.93
YEAST	0.10%	$1.90
CHOLINE CHLORIDE	0.15%	$0.48
NATURAL PRESERVATIVES	0.04%	$18.30

Both these foods, and most dog foods, use meat or chicken meals rather than the actual meats or chicken. A meal is a dry product, and comes in a bag. It is easy to transport, store, and use.

Most mammal and poultry tissues (the meats) are between 50 and 75% moisture. To make a meal, the meat is ground into small particles, then cooked for hours in the rendering vat. The liquid fat that rises to the top is drawn off to be sold separately as animal fat (this is the ingredient that may contain pentobarbital, see Part Three, Chapter 9) The remaining protein/water mixture is then dried into the final meat product, a powder. It takes about 3.5 pounds to 4 pounds of meat or chicken to make 1 pound of meat or chicken meal. If the manufacturer is paying 10 cents per pound for meat meal, the actual cost of the wet meat, before being made into the meal, is about 3 cents per pound. Chicken meal at 26 cents per pound is equivalent to 7 cents per pound fresh chicken. You get what you pay for.

Meat meals must be preserved, often with strong, human-synthesized preservatives like ethoxyquin. If the manufacturer of the dog food buys meal that contains ethoxyquin, and does not add any additional ethoxyquin, the manufacturer does not have to list it on the label.

CHAPTER 9
Toxins in Meats

In recent years many articles and books have documented the low quality meat sources that are used in many popular premium dog foods.

PENTOBARBITOL

Ann Martin's book, Foods Pet Die For, showed that dead dogs and cats were being used as ingredients in dog food.[1] The Animal Protection Institute's study, "What's Really in Pet Foods" documented the poor quality meats (4D—dead, dying, diseased or downed) and fats used.[2] In 1998, FDA tests found pentobarbital (from euthanized animals) in many dry dog foods, including some "premium" brands.[3]

In May 2003 Bovine Spongiform Encephalopathy (BSE) or Mad Cow Disease was found in a cow in Canada. The eight-year-old cow showed signs of illness, was sent to slaughter, and was condemned by the Alberta Agriculture authorities to be unfit for human consumption. Brain tissue was sent for testing and the remains of the cow were sent for rendering.[4] The cow ended up in dog food, produced in Canada and sold in the United States.[5]

Some dry dog food companies have worked hard to prevent dead dogs and cats and pentobarbital from being in their pet foods. We know this is true with most of the "super-premium" top line products. We don't know how the brands that sell retail for 25 cents per pound can avoid it—their ingredient costs dictate buying the lowest costs meats possible. Recently developed tests allow very specific DNA testing of foods. Cat and dog DNA has not been found. However, the roots of the pentobaribtol issue may be more that downer animals are often euthanized using this chemical. Typically producers of pet food simply rely on a letter or certification from the rendering plant that no pet carcasses are included in the meat meal, and do not test themselves.

HIGH TEMPERATURE COOKING CREATES CARCINOGENS

We noted in the last chapter that dog foods are processed at high temperatures and under high pressures. We saw that this processing reduces nutrition. High temperature processing also creates sub-stances—including heterocyclic amines and acrylamides—that are known to cause cancer in rodents and monkeys. Both of these substances are being intensively studied throughout the world as human carcinogens.

HETEROCYCLIC AMINES

Cooking meats, fish, and other foods, including wheat gluten, at high heat can form heterocyclic aromatic amines, which are extremely potent carcinogens:[6,7] "Heterocyclic aromatic amines are among the most potent mutagentic (substances that cause DNA mutations) sub-stances ever tested."[8]

Unfortunately, they are found in most dry dog foods. In a 2003 study, 13 out of 14 commercial dog foods tested by scientists at Lawrence Livermore National Laboratory contained heterocyclic amines and 24 of 25 tested contained other potent mutagens.[9]

The authors concluded "From these findings it is hypothesized that there is a connection between dietary heterocyclic amines and cancer in animals consuming these foods."[10]

CHAPTER 10
Toxins in "Animal Feed" Quality Minerals

Most people that have given thought to dog food understand that inexpensive dog foods must use inexpensive ingredients; especially low quality, human-waste product meats. What we didn't expect, though, is that "animal feed grade" minerals used to fortify the food may come from industrial waste products and include dioxins. In 2003, the FDA found dioxins, a product that dogs would never have been exposed to before the industrial revolution, in minerals that are used in animal feeds.[1] According to a story in the USA Today, "It is common practice to take industrial waste and use its byproducts in animal feeds." In this case, American Brass Company sold mineral-rich industrial waste to a company that produces mineral supplements for animal feeds.[2] The minerals produced contained dioxins. Exposure to dioxins is cumulative; the damage adds up in the body. The Food and Drug Administration (FDA), in an article about dioxins in animal feed grade minerals, states "with cumulative exposure, they are potential carcinogens and may cause reproductive or developmental health problems."[3]

Avoidance of dioxins is most important for pregnant dogs and young dogs. At Dioxin 2003, an international conference on effects of dioxins, many reports indicated that relatively low-dose exposures to dioxins in the womb or shortly after birth could irreparably damage an animal's reproductive and nervous systems.[4]

CHAPTER 11

The Dangerous Toxins and Allergens in Grains

Not only are grains high in carbohydrates and a poor source of protein, the less than human-edible (animal feed grade) grains used in almost all dry dog foods come with allergens, and some very deadly toxins, including mycotoxins. In addition, cooking high carbohydrate foods at high temperature may create acrylamides, another potential carcinogen. Grains may cause the most long-term harm of all the major ingredients in commercial dry dog food.

THE LONG STORAGE TIMES OF LOW COST GRAINS

Less than human-edible grains are by-products from the flour mills. These grains are the leftovers after the grains for human consumption are processed. It's the proverbial "separating the wheat from the chaff." People get the wheat, dogs the chaff. Most dog foods use mill run flour: the bottom of the storage elevator, the fines and broken kernels.

This flour is of lower value than flours going into the human food stream; therefore it gets reduced priority in handling. The more expensive grains are handled first. The lower cost grains, including low cost human-edible grains and pet food grade grains, are handled last. Therefore there is much longer "set time" for these products than the top-of-the-line products. Set time allows storage mites, insects, and worst of all, molds, to grow.

STORAGE MITES AND SKIN ALLERGIES

Atopic Dermatitis (skin allergies) is common in dogs.[1] In some geographic areas, perhaps as much as 15% of the canine population may suffer from Atopic Dermatitis.[2] Purebreds and mixed breeds appear to suffer equally from this sometimes debilitating problem.

Recent studies in peer-reviewed veterinary studies worldwide show that the consumption of the carcasses of storage mites that are in the grains used in dog foods may be a major contributing factor in symptoms of allergies in dogs.

The study of storage mites is relatively new, with much of the science developed in Europe in the last decade, examining the storage mite problems in processed human foods. We first learned about storage mites and skin allergy problems with dogs and cats from Dr. Patricia White of the Atlanta Allergy Clinic during her presentation at the Western Veterinary Conference 2003. Dr. White recommends canned or home cooked food for allergic dogs, not dry food. One of the causes of allergy symptoms, she speculates, is storage mites.[3]

Many dogs, like many people, have allergy problems. For numerous reasons, their immune systems are unable to handle the environment in which they live. Some of these reasons are simple to understand. Our closed houses filled with artificial components overload our systems with substances that are difficult for our bodies to process. Highly processed, inappropriate food does not provide our bodies with the tools for a healthy immune system. Exposure to environmental toxins and inappropriate foods sets the stage for our immune systems to become dysfunctional. Other reasons for allergic problems are not yet understood. Were people or dogs with allergies born with weak immune systems? Did they inherit a genetic tendency toward these problems from a parent? Was it malnutrition or exposure to toxins or specific allergens when in the womb? Science is just beginning to find answers to these questions.

Symptoms of allergies appear at threshold levels. Most people and most dogs can handle low levels of most allergens with little problem. But when we are allergic, and exposed to a lot of things that we're allergic to, we have symptoms. Generally, if we have some level of problem, the more allergens we're exposed to, the more allergy symptoms we have. If our immune systems work well, we have no problems. It's the same with dogs, except the allergy symptoms often show on the skin, with hot spots, hair loss, constant generalized itching, licking of paws, and other skin and coat problems.

Many people with allergies, and most with asthma, are allergic to the carcass and waste products of dust mites. Our modern homes, always warm and often humid, are ideal breeding grounds for these microscopic creatures. Warm, comfortable beds and couches are not quite their evolutionary bedrooms! A Japanese study, published in 2002 in a peer-reviewed Japanese veterinary journal, concluded that "antigens of house dust mites may be a major allergen in canine AD (Atopic Dermatitis)."[4]

Storage mites are cousins of the dust mite. Storage mites feed on grain; they seem to prefer the broken grains used in dog foods, and particularly love the mold that feeds on less than human-edible grains. When molds are under stress—being eaten by predators—they secrete the most deadly mycotoxins. When grains are processed into dog food, the carcass of the storage mite remains in the product. Storage mite contamination is unavoidable, even in human food in Europe, where the standards for many contaminants are much stricter. In 1996, 22% of cereal-based human foods tested in England had storage mites, and 38% of the cereal-based foods had storage mites after six weeks storage.[5]

Consumption of storage mite carcasses, we're learning, may be major cause of the symptoms of skin allergies in dogs. In a study by Dr. Larry Arlian et al published in the *American Journal of Veterinary Research*, January 2003, 94% of 84 dogs with Atopic Dermatitis had serum IgE against storage mite antigens. He concluded: "Storage mite sensitivity in dogs may be as important, if not more important, than dust mite sensitivity."[6] A French study, also published in 2002, showed that 120 of 150 dogs with Atopic Dermatitis tested positive for the antigen to either a species of storage mites, dust mites, or both.[7] These studies make sense to us. Dry dog foods are mostly grain, made with low cost, low priority grains with long set times—ideal breeding grounds for storage mites and molds.

Storage mites can be in the ingredients used in the dry pet foods, or can be a result of cross-contamination with raw ingredients in the dog food plant after the food was made. Keeping storage mites out of a dog food plant is just as difficult, if not more so, than keeping flies and spiders out of the plant. It's not possible, even with frequent fumigations of the pet food plants. The storage mites can also come from the way dog food is handled in the home. Storage mites like crumbs. For those who use containers or bins to store dry pet foods, we suggest washing the bin with warm soapy water after every bag of dry dog food is finished. Keep the food dry. Storage mites, like the deadly mycotoxin-producing molds we'll discuss in the next section, like moist environments.

We urge people that have dogs with skin allergies to work with diet before giving your dog steroids. If a grain-free diet works, your dog won't need steroids and his immune system will have a chance to recover. As the gut gets healthier, the immune system is better able to function. Steroids have serious long-term side effects that may shorten the life of your dog.

CARCINOGENS IN LOW QUALITY GRAINS

Did Mycotoxins Kill Zach? In Chapter 5, we saw that the dog's natural diet contained quadrillions x10^4 of bacteria of many species. Dogs, for the most part, are well equipped to handle bacteria in their food. Now we're going to look at another microbe, fungi. Specifically, we'll look at molds that feed on grain. Some of the waste products of these molds, called mycotoxins, are increasingly being implicated as long-term causes of cancer and other health problems in humans, poultry, pigs, and other animals worldwide.

For more complete information about mycotoxins and the risks they pose to human and animal health, we refer readers to the January 2003 report, *Mycotoxins: Risks in Plant, Animal, and Human Systems.* This report, published by the Council for Agricultural Science and Technology (CAST), an international consortium of 37 scientific and professional societies, represents the latest and best knowledge about mycotoxins. It is available on line at www.cast-science.org.

The consumption of mycotoxins is unavoidable if a dog eats a grain-based dog food. We'll document that long term ingestion of low levels of mycotoxins leads to cancer (including the splenic cancer that killed Zach) and other health problems.

Fungi, Molds, and Mycotoxins. Fungi are any of numerous chiefly parasitic plants that constitute the division Fungi. Fungi lack true chlorophyll. Unlike green plants, which use carbon dioxide and light as sources of carbon and energy, fungi meet these two requirements by assimilating organic matter. Carbohydrates are the preferred nutrient source of many fungi.[8]

Fungi can be found in air, in soil, on plants, and in water. Thousands, perhaps millions, of different types of fungi exist on Earth. The dangers of fungi are well known in the plant world. "Plants are attacked by bacteria and viruses, nematode worms, and insects, but fungi cause more plant diseases than all other enemies combined."[9] The most familiar fungi are mushrooms, yeast, mold, and mildew. We find molds in our bathrooms, kitchens, basements; all areas where there is a lot of humidity. Mold spores are the most prevalent microbe in air and cause many people allergy problems.[10] Allergies, though, are just the tip of the iceberg of the problems that molds can cause humans and animals.

Molds commonly grow on foods when the conditions, primarily the moisture level, are right. Two common molds are the blue-green mold on bread left too long in the refrigerator and the pink mold growing on ears of corn standing uncut in wet fields. Some of the waste products of these molds are toxic and are called mycotoxins.

Fungi are adept at producing a wide array of toxins that protect the fungi from bacteria, viruses, storage mites and other forms of life. For example, the *Penicillium* species produces the antibiotic Penicillin to protect itself from bacteria. Several other mycotoxins produced by this mold are potent carcinogens. Most molds produce more than one type of mycotoxin.

The total number of mycotoxins is not known, but potentially could number in the thousands.[11] New mycotoxins are being discovered at a high rate.[12] The major classes of mycotoxins with which we need to be concerned in dry dog foods are aflatoxins, trichothecenes (includes deoxynivalenol (DON) or vomitoxin), fumonisins, zearalenone, ochratoxin A, and ergot alkaloids.

Modern farming techniques are partly responsible for the increasing mycotoxin problem. Any activity that disturbs the stability of an ecosystem will increase the production of mycotoxins. Such activities include the widespread use of fertilizers and pesticides, high yielding plant varieties and the cultivation of a limited number of plant species with restricted genetic variation.[13]

"The use of crop culture practices in the United States that minimize tillage is increasing. Increased crop residues on the ground provide more fungal inoculants and create a more favorable environment for *Fusarium* growth. This increases the likelihood that cereal grains and their milling by-products used in pet foods will be contaminated with *Fusarium* toxins."[14] *Fusarium* molds produce vomitoxin.

An Ongoing Problem with Dry Dog Foods. In the last chapter, we looked at what could happen if a housefly carrying a spore of the *Aspergillus* mold lands on an open bag of dry dog food in a humid climate. Small amounts of aflatoxin-contaminated food may be consumed.

Even without the fly, mycotoxins will most likely already be in bags of dry dog food, especially those using less than human-edible grains. As we'll see, mycotoxins are unavoidable given the ingredients used in dry dog foods. Many mycotoxins, including aflatoxin and vomitoxin, survive the extrusion process. The cooking kills the mold, but does not remove the endotoxins produced by the mold.

Mycotoxin problems are not new to the dry dog food world. There have been many documented deaths and health problems of dogs from eating mycotoxin-contaminated grain-based foods. Aflatoxin poisoning has been documented in dogs since 1952[15] and has been a problem in dry dog food since dry food was developed.[16] A March 2003 article in the *Journal of the American Veterinary Association* summarized the issue of aflatoxin:

> "Despite these numerous studies, aflatoxicosis continues to be a problem in dogs. Since 1975, at least 11 major episodes have been documented, with the most recent and widespread episode in 1998. In that episode, 17 brands of commercial food formulated for dogs, all of which were produced by the same manufacturer, were contaminated with aflatoxin.... Fifty-five dogs died from eating the contaminated food, but it is likely that many more went unreported.... At the time of the episode, it was estimated that the company's sales accounted for one fourth of all food commercially prepared for dogs that was sold in Texas."[17]

Aflatoxin is not just a problem with dogs. It is estimated that 20,000 people per year die of liver cancer caused by aflatoxin.[18]

Vomitoxin-contaminated dog food has also been a serious problem. For example, in 1995 one of the leading premium brand dry dog and cat foods recalled 16,000 tons of product and received 11,000 phone calls from unhappy pet owners. Many of the calls came from dogs that refused to eat the product or that had vomiting and diarrhea problems. The problem stemmed from moldy wheat which contained 34 parts per million of vomitoxin, a toxin produced by Fusarium molds.[19]

The dog food companies settled their claims in this vomitoxin incident, and the furor died down. Few people looked at the long-term effects of ingestion of the mycotoxins despite this fact:

"The impact of fungal toxins on animals extends far beyond the obvious effect of causing death. The increased disease incidence because of immune system suppression, subtle damage to vital body organs, and interferences with reproduction is many times greater than that of immediate morbidity and lethality."[20]

Ever-present Mycotoxins. If one eats grain, one cannot avoid consuming some mycotoxins. "To reiterate, mycotoxins are essentially unavoidable in commodities."[21]

"DON (vomitoxin) is a natural metabolite produced by various members of the genus *Fusarium*. These fungi grow on various grains and are ubiquitous."[22]

Mycotoxins have been reported in almost all grains (wheat, corn, rice, barley, oats), peanuts, soybeans, nuts, and many other foods. The lower the cost of the grain, the more likely it is that the grain will have significant mycotoxin contamination. "Commercial dry extruded pet foods may contain large quantities of grain and grain by-products, and grain by-products may contain concentrated amounts of DON." [23]

In the USA, the FDA regulates the amounts of four myco-toxins, aflatoxins, DON, fumonisins, and patulins, allowed in human food and animal feed. "Small amounts of these contaminants may be legally permitted in foods and feeds because they are not entirely eliminated by good agricultural practices and good manufacturing practices...." [24] International standards differ. European standards are generally stricter and regulate more mycotoxins. As examples, we're going to look at the US standards for DON and fumonisins.

It has been reported that feed companies often blend mycotoxin-contaminated grains that exceed the standards with reduced—contaminated grains, thereby lowering the overall level of toxins in the feed to below the standard and allowing the grain to be used to feed animals, including dogs. [25]

For DON (vomitoxin) the FDA has set the following as "advisory levels":

FDA Advisory Levels for DON

1 ppm:
Finished wheat products for human consumption.

5 ppm:
All grains and grain by-products for swine and other animals (except cattle and chickens); these ingredients should not exceed 20% of the diet for swine and 40% for other animal species (including dogs). [26]

Let's compare the standards for humans and dogs. Humans are allowed 1 ppm (part per million) vomitoxin. Grain may constitute ⅓ or less of the human diet. On the other hand, feed for dogs is allowed five times that amount of vomitoxin, and grain may constitute ⅔ of the dog's diet. Is this too much vomitoxin?

Note that the allowable maximum percentage of grain in the diet for dogs is twice that for swine. We think the reason for this is that pig farmers keep good records and can determine cause and effect. Feed mycotoxins, lose production. Dog guardians don't see this. "Swine are recognized as the livestock species most susceptible to DON toxicity… but DON may be as toxic for dogs."[27]

Another example is the fumonisins class of mycotoxins. The fumonisins (B1 and B2 are the major ones) are the natural byproducts of the fungi *Fusarium* which contaminate corn. Even human-edible corn is susceptible to high levels of fumonisins. "The high incidence of fumonisins in corn-based products for human consumption, epidemiological investigations indicating a possible association… with esophageal cancer… and animal studies demonstrating the carcinogenicity of fumonisin B1 in rats, have heightened concerns about the public health impact of these contaminants."[28]

For total fumonisins, the FDA has proposed the following "guidance levels":

Human food product: 2–4 ppb
Pets: 10 ppb, not to exceed 50% of the diet.[29]

These are proposed guidance levels. Many dry dog foods, mostly low cost grocery and mass-merchandise brands, are more than 50% corn. Animal feed-quality corn, at about 5 cents per pound, is the lowest cost grain used in dog foods. (Animal feed quality wheat costs about 7 cents per pound.) Corn is particularly susceptible to contamination by mycotoxins including aflatoxins.

The North Carolina State University Mycotoxin Laboratory reported:

> "In a recent survey of suspect feed samples, some amount of aflatoxin, deoxynivalenol, or fumonisin was found in over 70 percent of the samples tested.... Fumonisin, a mycotoxin often associated with horse deaths, is thought to occur very frequently; however, its discovery is so recent that data on occurrence has not been established."[30]

Even if the standards were set much lower, as they are in Europe, it is not easy to detect mycotoxins. There are thousands of different mycotoxins and no single test for all the different compounds. One type of mold may produce many different mycotoxins. Molds grow in lumps, not evenly diffused throughout the bin of grain. For example, there may be only one aflatoxin-contaminated kernel in a bin. Even the most quality conscious manufacturer cannot test every kernel. "It is difficult to estimate accurately and precisely the mycotoxin concentration in a large bulk lot because of the large variability associated with the overall mycotoxin test procedure."[31]

If you're feeding your dog a corn-based food, your dog is consuming fumonisins, and probably aflatoxins. Peanuts are often contaminated with aflatoxins, and used as a source of fiber in "diet" foods. If it's a wheat-based food, she is consuming vomitoxin. All grains can be contaminated with mycotoxins. Typically, several mycotoxins may be present in contaminated food. For example, combinations of aflatoxin, trichothecenes, and fumonisins have been found as simultaneous contaminants in corn.[32]

Heat Resistant Mycotoxins. Aflatoxins, vomitoxin and some other mycotoxins are considered to be heat stable,[33,34] though heat appears to reduce the toxicity of aflatoxins. Vomitoxin is also stable to conventional extrusion processing. Therefore if toxins are present in the ingredients used for manufacture, the toxins will be present in the food when packaged.[35] The high temperatures and pressures of the extrusion process destroy most of the actual molds, though some molds, including the *Aspergillus* mold that excretes aflatoxin, are heat resistant.[36]

And the Dog Eats the Mycotoxins. Studies have confirmed that dogs will eat mycotoxin-contaminated foods. Many dead and sick dogs, and bereft caretakers have been the result. Specific studies with vomitoxin showed that dogs do not start refusing vomitoxin contaminated foods until levels reach 4.5mg/kg of food (4.5 parts per million), almost at the allowable FDA limit for animal feed.[37]

What Happens When a Dog Consumes Mycotoxins.
Mycotoxicosis, the disease resulting from exposure to a mycotoxin, may be manifested as acute to chronic, and ranges from rapid death to tumor formation. More occult disease may occur when the mycotoxin interferes with immune processes, rendering the patient more susceptible to infectious diseases.[38]

Health problems from bacteria and mycotoxins are different. Bacteria fit our definition of an enemy much better than molds do. A battle with bacteria happens soon after infection. It gets our attention. When you or your dog has a bacterial problem, one dies or gets stronger. If we survive, we may have built resistance to those bacteria. The battle revs up our immune system.

Mycotoxin problems are much different. Consumption of mycotoxins may kill quickly. But much more often mycotoxins kill slowly, suppressing the immune system, creating long-term health problems in all organs of the body.[39,40] Unlike battles with bacteria, your dog never gets stronger from the battle; mycotoxins leave internal scars. The effects of mycotoxins are cumulative. A little bit here, a little bit there—and five years later the dog may die of cancer.

ACRYLAMIDES

In the last chapter, we documented that many dog foods contain worrisome amounts of heterocyclic amines, a very potent carcinogen caused by high temperature cooking of meats. Another potential carcinogen in dog foods, acrylamides, is caused by the high temperature cooking of carbohydrates.

Scientists in Europe in 2002 discovered that high carbohydrate foods cooked at high temperatures may contain acrylamides, a class of carcinogens. They found that some everyday foods, including extruded breakfast cereals, contained high levels of acrylamides, while boiled and raw foods appear to have no acrylamides.[41]

Dry dog food is a high carbohydrate food cooked at high temperature. We think that since the ingredients of dog food are largely those that are susceptible to this problem, and since the cooking process is very similar to those that cause the problem, it's very likely that dry pet foods contain acrylamides. We have not seen reliable data.

PART THREE
Conclusion

In Part Two we saw that dry dog food does not provide the proper macro and micronutrients for dogs to be at their best. In this Part, we documented that if your dog is eating dry dog food, especially those made with low-cost grains, which may have been stored for a long time, then she is probably consuming mycotoxins, heterocyclic amines, acrylamides, and storage mites. If your dog has a genetic predisposition to cancer, or suffered from malnutrition or exposure to toxins in the womb, or was weaned early at a young age onto a food that contained storage mites or mycotoxins, then these allergens and carcinogens may create long-term problems for her. Even for dogs (and humans) that have not encountered any of these problems, long term exposure to these toxins has been proven to be detrimental to health.

In Part Four we'll see how easy it is to improve this situation, while, if financially necessary, still feeding some dry dog food.

PART FOUR
Improving the Odds is Easy

It is never too late to improve the odds that your dog will live a long, healthy life. Studies with fruit flies, rats, and humans (specifically following the unification of East and West Germany) show that age-specific death rates are strongly influenced by current conditions and behaviors.[1] In other words, if you have an overweight, sedentary dog, you can immediately improve the odds that she'll live a long life by starting her on a proper diet and exercise program.

There are six chapters to this part. Even though this book is primarily about nutrition, we place almost equal weight on all the chapters.

Some people may try to protect their dogs from all dangers, or feel guilty if they do not succeed all the time. We urge you to let your dogs have fun, play and enjoy life. A dog that enjoys life will be better able to overcome exposure to inappropriate foods and toxins than an unhappy dog. We can't protect our dogs, or ourselves,

from everything. Every tiny step helps. A little improvement here and a little improvement there can go a long way. It all adds up.

A healthy dog starts with a healthy mother. The most important time (for the puppies) to follow the suggestions in this section is from several months before mating, continuing until the puppies are weaned These are crucial times for the bitch to be fed a highly nutritious meat-based diet, and to avoid toxins and storage mites. A pregnant dog fed a highly nutritious diet will have puppies that live longer, healthier lives than the puppies from mothers fed average diets. We think it is especially important for young puppies to eat raw meat and other raw foods. Raw foods may help the puppy develop a full complement of normal bacteria that may help ward off bacterial problems in the future.[2] Of course, we'd also like you to continue to feed that mom well after the puppies are weaned, helping her replace what she used to make those puppies—and to support her on into a long and healthy life of her own.

A proper education is essential for a dog to live a full life. A well-educated dog can go more places, have more fun, and be with her human much more often than a dog without good social skills. It's worth the investment in time.

CHAPTER 12
Improve Nutrition

We feel strongly that a varied, fresh food diet is the best way to provide our animals with the tools to enjoy vibrant health. We all know that this is true with humans. For some people, providing a full-time fresh raw diet for their dogs (and cats) may be too expensive or time-consuming to consider. They can still do a lot to improve the nutrition of their dog.

The more we can reduce the impact of the grain and the lack of natural forms of micronutrients in dry dog food by adding fresh meats and vegetables, the better. We must always keep in mind, though, that dogs need the proper amounts and balance of nutrients, including calcium (Ca), from the bone, and phosphorous (P), from the bone and the meat. Adding too much real food to the diet without considering Ca, P and other minerals may lead to skeletal problems. We've therefore divided our recommendations into two "steps":

Adding select "table scraps" to dry food, up to a total of 15% of the diet;

Feeding proper raw diets as a base, and adding dry food if necessary to reduce the overall cost.

The third section of this chapter discusses foods to avoid feeding your dogs (or cats).

Adding juiced or finely chopped vegetables is a must. Only fresh vegetables and fruits have proven cancer-fighting and anti-aging properties. A diet rich in fruits and vegetables may also help protect your dog's brain against aging and may help keep your old dog from acting old.[1]

ADDITIONS TO DRY FOOD—UP TO 15% OF DIET

For almost no cost and little effort you can improve the odds that your dog will live a long life. The most important thing to understand is that the advice "never feed people food or table scraps to your animals" is out-of-date and directly harmful to you dogs and cats. Would we feed our children nothing but dry food in a bag? Are dogs and cats different?

Give your dog people food. Just prepare the food right, and don't overdo it. There is a balance of nutrients that is optimal for your dog. Therefore, when adding table scraps, limit the quantity to about 15% by weight table scraps. Here's what we recommend, with a discussion below on each type of ingredient recommended.

Steve's Nutrition Booster

Juice or finely chop raw **vegetables**, like broccoli stalks. Add small pieces of **raw meat**. Crush a few **nuts**. Add a small quantity of high-quality oils containing **omega-3 fatty acids**. Pour the mixture on top of the dry or canned food.

Vegetables and Fruits. Give your dogs bright green vegetables like broccoli stalks, dark green lettuce outer leaves, and asparagus spear stalks, several times a week. Green vegetables contain chlorophyll.

Natural chlorophylls exert protective effects against carcinogen exposure in animals and people.[2,3] Human studies in China show that chlorophyll may help delay the onset of symptoms of liver cancer caused from aflatoxin-contaminated grains.[4]

For the most micronutrients for your dollar, juice or finely chop a broccoli stalk. The stalk has just as much nutrition as the broccoli flower, and is often thrown away. It contains many important cancer fighting nutrients. Remember when feeding vegetables to break the cell walls of the vegetable by juicing or finely chopping. A rigid cell wall, composed of cellulose and other polymers, surrounds plant cells. Cellulose is very difficult for dogs to digest. It is the contents of the cell itself, not the cellulose wall, which provides most of the nutrition.[5] When the ancestral dog ate the guts of animals and fish, and the raw scraps tossed to the dogs by ancestral humans, the dog consumed the partially digested plant matter that the animal or fish ate. A rabbit, for example, would have finely masticated and broken the cell wall of the carrot.

If your dog grazes on grass that has not been sprayed with pesticides, herbicides or other poisons, it's fine (as long as she doesn't throw up on your carpet). Fresh grass provides chlorophyll, vitamin C and hundreds of other antioxidants and enzymes. Don't let your dog or cat eat grass that has been exposed to human-made chemicals. If the grass is in the woods, it's usually fine. If the grass is part of a farm or suburban "perfect lawn," try to prevent your dog from eating it.

Meat and Fish. Use the parts of the meat or fish that you do not want. If you're eating a steak, for example, give your dog the raw gristle. The gristle contains cartilage, a natural source of glucosamine.

The authors believe that raw Pacific salmon should not be fed to dogs. Some knowledgeable people, for whom the authors have great respect, believe that freezing salmon commercially, at temperatures below −20°C (−4°F) for at least 48 hours, makes the fish safe for dogs.

Pacific salmon often carry a worm, called a trematode, which itself carries a microbe, *Neorickettsia Hilmonthoeca*. The trematode lives in the intestine of many fish-eating birds and mammals (including cats), with little ill effect. Dogs, however, can get very sick and die from the microbe within the trematode. Deep freezing kills the trematode; we are not sure deep freezing kills the microbe (bacteria typically survive freezing) and therefore do not feed raw salmon to our dogs.[6]

High Quality Oils. Omega-3 fatty acids can be added in the form of fresh, good quality oils. Omega-3 sources from fish are best, although variety is important in oil as in all other food. Good choices include fish oil, salmon oil, flax oil, cod liver oil, and hemp oil. Choose cold-pressed, minimally processed oils when possible. The oils in many pet foods are not good sources of these nutrients because oils are extremely delicate and easily damaged by exposure to air. Keep these oils refrigerated. Oils are very concentrated, so add only small amounts to keep the nutrients in balance.

Adding too much oil without additional antioxidants, especially natural sources of vitamin E, can have long-term detrimental effects. "Short-term benefits of high essential fatty acid (EFA) intake may be found concurrent with insidious effects leading to long-term toxicities if antioxidant status is insufficient."[7]

There is a considerable anecdotal evidence (consisting of reports or observations, not peer-reviewed scientific studies) that adding omega-3 fatty acids can reduce the symptoms of skin allergies.[8] We think that these results are due to the addition of needed, whole food nutrition, not a medicinal or therapeutic result: missing food was added, and the body knows what to do with it.

We think adding small amounts of omega-3 fatty acids is especially important during pregnancy. Dietary sources generally do not provide sufficient omega-3s for optimum long-term health of the fetus. Recent studies support this approach. A 2003 study published in the *Journal of Nutrition* concluded that fish oil supplementation of rats during pregnancy reduces adult disease risk in their offspring.[9] Another 2003 study showed that consumption of omega-3 fatty acids during pregnancy might help prevent allergies in babies born to women with a history of allergies.[10]

Nuts and Other foods. We recommend giving dogs, from time to time, ground nuts. Nuts, especially walnuts, contain high quality oils, a variety of tocopherols (types of vitamin E), trace minerals, including selenium, and hundreds of natural antioxidants. For treats, we often use cashews.

Well-washed avocado skins are a good source of folic acid and other nutrients, and free. It's the natural food relationship between humans and dogs. The human eats the flesh of the avocado, the dog the skin. Raw honey, added in small quantities once a week, (for a Chihuahua this might be three drops...) has powerful antioxidants and other health benefits.

Feeding Raw Ground Bones. Ground raw chicken and turkey necks are excellent foods. Bones provide a lot of nutrition, including fat and a natural source of calcium and phosphorous, which may help keep dogs lean.[11] The cartilage provides a natural source of glucosamine. We do recommend, for most dogs, that the bones be ground for the safest application.

BeeBop, Zach's granddaughter, starting eating the raw meat off whole turkey necks when she was three weeks old. The puppies had no teeth; they would gnaw on them. It was fun to watch them. A turkey neck would keep the litter of puppies busy for hours, and gave them good jaw exercise. When the puppies were three weeks old, each one was given a raw chicken wing first thing in the morning. This kept them occupied and allowed Steve to make coffee before having to deal with them. This litter now, as adults, eats turkey necks and chicken wings differently than the other adult dogs, who were first introduced to raw bones as adults. BeeBop eats the neck carefully, picking it apart, slowly eating the entire neck. Her mother, Daisy, who first ate turkey necks as an adult, gulps the necks down.

Many highly respected veterinarians (for example Dr. T. J. Dunn, a Wisconsin veterinarian who has been recommending raw diets for decades)[12] do not recommend giving whole raw bones to dogs. There is a small risk. Our advice, after speaking with many holistic and traditional veterinarians, is to grind the raw bones, unless your dog was introduced to whole raw bones at a very young age, like BeeBop was. Ask your butcher to grind the bones or buy a grinder.

Note: please remember to handle raw meats intended for dogs as you would any raw product and any canned or dry dog food: Keep away from small children, and wash all utensils and the dog's food bowl in warm soapy water after use.

Let's quickly look at the nutrition we just added. From a micronutrient point of view, we added nutrients in their natural forms (selenomethione for example); natural, complete forms of antioxidants, thousands of different types of phytonutrients, and many different types of food enzymes. We've improved the macronutrient content by increasing protein and quality fats, and thereby reducing the percentage of carbohydrate in the diet. We've added taurine and L-carnitine. And we've accomplished this at almost no cost.

Remember to reduce the amount of dry or canned dog food you feed accordingly.

FEEDING PROPER RAW DIETS

The more fresh foods we feed our dogs the better—as long as the food provides all the nutrients in the right balances: The pet food regulators call this "complete and balanced." When foods we add to dry food exceed more than 15 to 20% by weight, we must be careful that we are keeping the nutrients, particularly the Ca and P, in balance. For example, feeding too much meat without the bone will lead to serious skeletal problems. Adding a lot of fat without increasing the micronutrient levels of the food may also lead to malnutrition problems. The dog may become full, having consumed a lot of calories, and stop eating before consuming a sufficient amount of micronutrients. Dogs with undetected problems could develop pancreatitis if fed more fat than they can handle, though this happens more often with cooked fat than with raw.

We believe, when economically possible, dogs should be fed at least 50% a balanced raw diet and at most 50% properly-handled dry food. To do this, one must either purchase a commercially prepared raw dog food, or learn to make a proper raw diet. If you purchase a commercial product, you can still add Steve's nutrition booster to reduce overall costs.

If you feed your dogs frozen foods, we recommend that you defrost the food in the refrigerator, or warm it up with the use of a double cooker. Recent studies show that microwaving may destroy more of the antioxidants than other methods of heating food.[13]

If you want the absolute best nutrition for your dog, you need to feed fresh foods full time. Proper raw diets help keep your dog healthy, which may save you money in the long run. If you have several dogs, you may want to learn to make your own dog food, at least some of the time.

For dogs with health problems (allergies, arthritis, or any immune related problem), we recommend full time feeding of balanced raw diets. Quite often, feeding a raw diet full time will solve the problem. We have known very few ill dogs who could not handle the switch; most frequently improvement is quickly seen. With these dogs, a reduction in expense is often seen quickly— food is expensive, but not as expensive as all of the medical help that was needed to support a sick animal.

Evaluating Commercial Raw Diets. We have formulated and sold some of the leading commercial raw diets for dogs. We have some strong opinions about what makes an excellent raw diet. In this section we try to give you sufficient information to understand what may be best for your animal.

There are some excellent commercial raw diets on the market, and some very poor diets. The rapidly growing trend of feeding dogs raw diets has brought in some less than scrupulous and less than knowledgeable "manufacturers" of raw diets. It is easy to tell the difference between the good and the bad, if you do your homework. It's worth learning enough to make a well-educated choice.

We strongly recommend feeding only human-edible raw foods. Some companies use less than human-edible meats; we don't agree with this practice. Indeed, the F.D.A. Center for Veterinary Medicine issued model guidelines for raw pet diet manufacturers. The guidelines recommended the use of human-edible ingredients.

The excellent raw diet manufacturers, in our opinion, combine knowledge of modern canine nutritional science with an understanding of the ancestral diets of dogs. The labels on their packages have an AAFCO complete and balanced statement (or Canadian equivalent). Their foods are tested for micronutrient content, and the companies provide, upon request, a complete nutrient profile. Most of the micronutrients come from vegetables and fruits, not human-synthesized vitamins and minerals.

The quality companies also provide technical support to you and your veterinarian. We urge you to ask the manufacturer tough questions. Be sure the manufacturer understands dogs and nutrition. Ask to see a complete nutrient profile, preferably determined through chemical analyses and not just calculated on a spreadsheet. The ideal product would be well tested with at least 3 generations of dogs, but currently most well-made raw diets have not been in production this long.

The "AAFCO complete and balanced" statement, or Canadian equivalent, on the package is a positive sign that the manufacturer has, at least, thought about the micronutrient content required by the pet food regulators. It is not a sure sign that the micronutrients are present, though. Some manufacturers may not test their food for all the micronutrients.

The worst products we've seen are made by companies that are jumping into the market with little knowledge of, or even concern for, dogs. We've seen some products made and sold by meat processors who add in much of their fat trim waste from other products.

We've seen products on the market, without any bone or other mineral sources, that state, in their feeding directions, "add Calcium to balance the high Phosphorous levels in the meat." These companies do not understand that the major source of Phosphorus is from bone, not meat. They also do not understand the importance of proper balance of Calcium and Phosphorus. We strongly recommend avoiding their products. The average customer may not know enough to spot these differences and we have seen some very ill dogs as a result of improper use of these products.

COMPLETE	NOT COMPLETE
AAFCO COMPLIANT: Guaranteed to provide a minimum of all the nutrients that modern canine nutritional science considers necessary for all life stages.	**NOT AAFCO COMPLIANT:** Put the pieces together to design your own complete diet.
Meat, bone, and vegetables: Cubes, tubs, chubs, and patties. Recipes vary widely, including various fruits and vegetables. Percentages of meat and bone may be very different depending on the opinion of manufacturer. Supplementation may be with chemically synthesized vitamins. **Best Choice:** micronutrients from whole foods, human edible ingredients. **Meat and bone and supplements:** Widely varying formulas: The bone puts this food one big step up from the ones below. **Meat alone and supplements:** Without the bone and vegetables: these do not contain natural sources of Ca, P and other minerals and vitamins. Not a good choice. **BEST CHOICE!** Human-edible ingredients, balance of meat, bone, vegetables and fruit reflecting natural diet. Variety is important.	**Meat and vegetables: — NOT complete.** Various formulations, may or may not contain bone, but not AAFCO compliant. May be useful as supplements up to 15% of diet. **Separate components:** May be single or mixed meats, with or without bone, vegetables and fruit. These products may be of excellent quality, but are meant to be fed as part of a feeding program, not as a complete food. May be useful as supplement up to 15% of diet. Minerals, oils, calcium and other supplements sometimes sold to complete the food. **Note: Claims of organic, free range, human edible etc. in any category of pet food should be examined with care. Learn the subtleties of reading labels. If products actually are of this quality, price will reflect ingredients!**

"The best looking dogs I've ever seen are on good raw diets. The worst looking dogs I've ever seen are on bad raw diets." —*Dr. Karen Becker, Natural Pet Animal Hospital, Tinley Park*

An increasing number of people are making fresh food diets for their dogs and cats. When done properly, homemade dog foods are very nutritious and tasty. We highly recommend them. There are several very good workbooks on the topic, and some which in our opinion are inaccurate or lacking in information. However, one of the most common problems we see is that people fail to read the whole book!

Evaluating Books on Making Dog Food. We recommend choosing workbooks which combine knowledge about the ancestral diet of dogs with thorough knowledge of the National Research Council recommended nutrient profiles for dogs (or the AAFCO nutrient profiles). Quality workbooks can be found at pet food stores which specialize in high quality foods and through select dog-related web sites.

When reviewing books on feeding dogs, we urge the reader to recall that the dog evolved at the garbage dump. The dog is not a true hunter like a wolf and does not need to be fed like a wolf. In addition, serving the same foods as the ancestral diet does not mean the dog is getting the same nutrients as the ancestral diet. Omega-3 fatty acids were more prevalent in ancestral foods than in modern foods; and wild animals and plants provided higher levels of micronutrients than those raised with modern farming methods.

Since one in three dogs will die of cancer, and only vegetables and fruits have proven cancer fighting properties, we recommend following diets which include lots of vegetables and fruits. Some ardent raw bone feeders question the role of vegetables and fruits. We don't. The natural diet of dogs contained some vegetable and fruit matter, and the nutrient profiles that 50 years of modern canine science has documented as essential (shown in the AAFCO nutrient profiles) can only be achieved through a minimum of 20 to 30% vegetables in a real food diet.

We advise the reader to avoid workbooks that recommend feeding mostly raw meaty bones. Too much bone can lead to absorption problems with other minerals, including zinc and copper, leading to long-term health problems. A diet very high in bone has led to severe constipation in some dogs. Bone also has a lot of fat: too much bone and not enough antioxidants can lead to long-term cellular damage. Avoid recipes which state "please add bone meal or eggshell powder." Bone meal and eggshell powder are two different things. The recipe should be specific. Bones, and bone meal, provide Ca and P. Eggshell powder is 98% calcium carbonate, and contains no P. Adding just Ca to an all meat and vegetable diet will create an unbalanced diet and may result in skeletal problems. The ratio of Ca to P, as well as the total amounts of Ca and P, are important.

Foods to Avoid. We recommend avoiding grains, potatoes, onions, raisins, grapes, chocolate, and, for some dogs, yeast products.

Potatoes are high in carbohydrates, and provide few micronutrients. In a review by the World Cancer Research Fund, potatoes were the only vegetable found not to help in reducing the risk of cancer.[14] Potatoes used for dog food may contain significant amounts of solanine, a potential toxin.[15]

Onions should not be fed to dogs. A compound in onions

inhibits normal enzyme activity in red blood cells, which may cause hemolytic anemia.

The ASPCA's Animal Poison Control Center database shows a trend in dogs that had eaten grapes or raisins toward acute kidney failure. The reason for this is unknown.[16] Although it's a rare occurrence, it's easy to avoid the risk.

Chocolate can be deadly for some dogs. Some dogs are sensitive to theobromine, a chemical contained in the cocoa bean. It has also been reported that dogs that ingest cocoa bean mulch (used as landscaping material) may exhibit symptoms of chocolate poisoning.[17] It's too bad that chocolate may hurt our dogs. Dark chocolate is delicious and nutritious for humans, and unfortunately, most dogs love it. The closest Steve has seen to death-by-chocolate was when Bogart, Zach's dad, ate four pounds of Godiva chocolate that Steve had foolishly left on the counter. When Steve came home from work, Bogart greeted him with a silly smile and gold wrapping all over his beard. The empty boxes and wrapping were strewn all over the floor. Bogart had unwrapped each piece! Four pounds of rich chocolate! Between fits of anger and laughter, Steve was ready to kill Bogart. Beth's brother's dog, on the other hand, suffered more serious consequences. He ate too many chocolate chips. He was on intravenous fluids at the veterinary hospital for three days with neurologic symptoms and organ toxicity—he was a lab who ate everything.

Some dogs are allergic to yeast products. If you give your dog any type of yeast (some people believe that brewers' yeast and garlic helps repel fleas), watch your dog carefully. We've found that dogs with a history of systemic problems like ear and skin irritations are likely to have an allergy to yeast and should stay away from it.

CHAPTER 13
Minimize Mycotoxin Consumption

As we saw in the last chapter, if we feed dry dog foods to our dogs, it is inevitable that they will consume mycotoxins. We can minimize the consumption of mycotoxins by minimizing grain consumption, and by handling dry dog food carefully. "Prepared feeds left for more than a day in feeding bins… are susceptible. Improper storage of foods fed to dogs and cats, such as poorly sealed products exposed to warm, moist, aerated conditions, may also lead to mold growth and aflatoxin contamination."[1]

It's all common sense. Would you leave your bread in a humid area, unprotected, for weeks on end? Would you buy five weeks worth of bread at one time? No, you wouldn't. Please don't do that with dry dog foods either.

The average dog guardian buys food once every 39 days[2] and, presumably, keeps the dog food bag open for 5 weeks. By the time the dog eats the food at the bottom of the bag, many of the micronutrients are lost; much of the fat has oxidized (become rancid and perhaps toxic); and mold and storage mites have had ample time to grow and multiply. In the last chapter we saw that after six weeks storage the number of human foods with storage mites almost doubled.

REDUCING PROBLEMS WITH DRY DOG FOODS

1. **Feed foods which use only human edible grains.**
Dog food manufacturers are prohibited by regulations
from mentioning on their labels that they use human-
edible ingredients. Knowledgeable pet food store
employees can guide you to the brands which use
human-edible grains. Expect to pay more: human-edible
grains will increase the cost of a dog food by at least 20%
to $1.25+ per pound for a 20 pound bag.

2. **Buy fresh bags of food.** Look for dates on the bags.
This is especially important in the summer. We don't
want to feed food that's been sitting in a hot Florida
warehouse for three months. The fresher the food, the
better it is.

3. **Buy small bags of food.** Given time, heat, and
humidity, fats oxidize, nutrition degrades, and storage
mites and molds grow. Use the bag as quickly as possible,
preferably in less than one week.

4. **Keep the food dry.** Even in waterproof containers,
dry dog food may get moist. When you open it, humid
air gets in. Test this yourself. Take a loaf of bread and
keep it in a dog food container for one month. See what
happens.

5. **Store dry food in the freezer to avoid many potential problems.**

6. **If the food looks or feels moist, throw it away** in an area the dogs can't get into. Do not let them eat it.

7. **If the food is off-color or has an off smell, toss it.**

8. **Do not buy bags of dog food that are torn.**

9. **If your dog says no, do not force her to eat.**

10. **If your dog acts strange after eating dry dog food take the dog and food to the veterinarian.**[3]

11. **Serve a variety of dry foods using different grains.** As we saw in the last chapter, corn is likely to be contaminated with fumonisins and wheat with vomitoxin. Serving a variety of dry foods using different grains minimizes the chances your dog will get a lot of one specific type of mycotoxin.

"Greater concern exists where populations depend on a single staple in the diet. If that staple is contaminated, consumers are exposed to greater amounts of the mycotoxin over a given period of time than populations that consume a wide variety of foods."[4]

Don't Let Your Dog Eat Moldy Garbage! We've heard of many dogs that got very sick after eating moldy garbage, including bread, macaroni, and dairy products.[5] We remember the days we used to toss old pieces of bread outside for the birds. It's probably okay during a cold winter, but, we know now, not a humid summer.

Moldy bread can kill dogs, quickly at times, or, more likely, five years later. We don't feed moldy bread to the birds anymore, either!

CHAPTER 14

Avoid Close-to-the-Ground Toxins

Dogs are low to the ground. Their noses are always at ground level, sniffing, tasting, eating, and drinking. They can find and consume human-made toxins which we often don't think about. What scares us most is water run-off from farmland or suburban lawns. This water may have high concentrations of toxins including pesticides and herbicides. These chemicals can be neurotoxic (poisonous to the nervous system, including the brain) and can cause cancer. This is not what you want your dog to drink.

Certain lawn chemicals and carpet cleaners are dangerous to dogs and cats. Our pets may absorb some of the chemicals through their pads. Speak with your local garden center, pet food store, or check web sites for advice on the use of non-toxic lawn chemicals and carpet cleaners. You can get a back issue of *The Whole Dog Journal*, May 2001, for a good discussion of lawn care products and November 2002 for carpet and floor cleaning products.[1] Do read the fine print on the label; we've heard of some dogs and cats that got quite sick after walking on carpet that was cleaned with supposedly "safe" carpet cleaners.

Pressure-treated wood decks contain arsenic that may be absorbed by dogs through their pads. Pressure treated wood (chromated copper arsenic) is no longer manufactured in the U.S. for residential use because the arsenic can rub off when touched. Most wooden decks in the U.S. are made of pressure-treated wood; we do not know the long-term effects of dogs absorbing the arsenic through their pads. Certainly it is most important to prevent dogs from chewing on pressure treated wood decks and picnic tables.

Flame retardants (polybrominated diphenyl ether—PBDE) are used in a products ranging from kid's pajamas to computers. A flame retardant may be especially dangerous to fetuses. These chemicals are similar to the PCBs (polychlorinated biphenyls) that were banned in the 1970s due to their toxicity. Products containing PBDE may release or outgas these chemicals.

If your dog is pregnant, keep her away from products containing flame retardants to the best of your ability. At an international meeting called Dioxin 2003, reports indicated that relatively low-dose exposures to PBDE in the womb or shortly after birth could irreparably damage an animal's reproductive and nervous systems.[2] *Do not use old pajamas or other similar products to line the pen when the puppies are born.*

Other toxins to watch out for include many plastic pet toys, bug bait, bug sprays, certain fertilizers, oil, snail bait, antifreeze, sidewalk and road salts, certain soaps, fabric and pot/pan coatings, burnt trash (may contain dioxins), flame retardants found in electrical appliances, building materials and household products… and many more. Many knowledgeable people consider some of the human-synthesized preservatives—ethoxyquin, BHA, BHT and others—to be poisons.

The dangers from many toxins are cumulative; every exposure weakens dogs. We have to let our dogs run and be dogs; but, at the same time, we have to watch close to the ground for human-made toxins and help our dogs avoid them. If your dog, once a month or so, drinks some run-off water, don't worry about it. If your dog drinks run-off water everyday, Danger Danger Danger.

CHAPTER 15

Minimize "Approved" Toxins

Consider that while many medications can be lifesavers, unnecessary use can be toxic. Awareness of the dangers of overuse of medication, including flea medication, is rising, but many people don't realize that because a medication is commonly used, it is not necessarily without risk.

EXTERNAL PARASITE TREATMENT

Many people and holistic veterinarians question the wisdom of using "spot-on" flea killers. The authors normally do not recommend spot-on flea killers, and highly recommend against the use of these products (or flea collars) for pregnant dogs.

Dr. Kathleen Dudley, in the *Journal of the American Holistic Veterinary Medical Association*, sums up the issue of spot-on flea killers succinctly: "When we attempt to get rid of our animals' fleas by utilizing chemicals that are toxic to the brain and nervous system, that may disrupt hormone (endocrine) systems, and that cause cancer, it's sort of like burning the house down to get rid of ants—effective, sure, but what are you left with?"[1]

The authors' dogs do not need flea killers. Good exercise and diet keep the fleas from becoming a problem. Before we started feeding good food, fleas were a continual problem. Yes, we were skeptical, but this has been our experience.

Mange cases are often recognized as arising from an immune system that's not up to the job due to environmental factors, which may include poor food. While harsh systemic treatment is often used for these problems, improved diet and other support of the immune system frequently resolves issues.

STEROIDS, ANTIBIOTICS, ANTI-INFLAMMATORY DRUGS

Steroids, antibiotics, and anti-inflammatory drugs (some examples are Rimadyl, aspirin, Etogesic) are commonly used to alleviate symptoms of arthritis, allergies, and other medical problems. Use of these drugs can be minimized if our animals are fed a proper, fresh food diet. All of these drugs have possible life threatening side effects, and veterinarians are aware that the long term use of steroids will shorten an animal's life.

Antibiotics are frequently used "just in case," or because "it can't hurt," Well, it can hurt. It's possible to do a culture to see what antibiotic is the proper one, but this is often not done in veterinary practice. Often the bacterial and fungal skin problems we see in allergic dogs are improved radically by simply washing the area frequently, rather than treating the skin with a systemic medication which alters the balance in the entire body. As diet helps the body to function better, these common problems usually diminish.

HEARTWORM PREVENTION

Using heartworm medication is, in our opinion, a personal choice. Beth has had a dog with heartworm and would not want to see another, but the use of this relatively safe chemical is better limited to the part of the year when heartworm transmission is possible. In most areas year round medication is not necessary or advisable. There is much good information about this topic on the website of the American Heartworm Society, www.heartwormsociety.org.

VACCINATIONS

How often to vaccinate is a hotly debated topic. Veterinary schools and associations no longer recommend routine yearly vaccination.

Veterinarians who vaccinate ill animals are in direct violation of the label recommendations. We suggest that you look into current recommendations and do some research for yourself on these topics. Ron Schultz, DVM has done much work in this area at the University of Wisconsin. In addition, BBC News in April 2004 carried an article entitled "Vets Issue Animal Vaccine Warning" stating that many vaccines given in yearly doses last much longer. We urge readers to speak to your veterinarian about minimizing vaccinations.

TAKE CHARGE OF THE HEALTH OF YOUR ANIMALS

These are a few of the topics we would like you to look into before you just use chemicals on your dog or cat. We know far too many animals permanently damaged by treatment of "disease" and exposure to unnecessary toxins. Are there other ways to treat this condition? Often there are, but you may need to seek out alternate veterinary advice to find them.

We do not mean to say that all veterinarians are using medication thoughtlessly; we know many veterinarians do a wonderful job. We do think that we, as consumers, have a responsibility to take charge of the health of our animals and learn enough to make informed choices.

While proper medication is always an issue to discuss with your veterinarian, most would agree that unnecessary use of drugs is to be avoided. Most would also agree that long term use of many drugs is harmful to overall health.

What many have not considered is that food can make enough of a difference for medication to be unnecessary.

CHAPTER 16
Keep Your Dog Lean

"Consumption of a low-calorie yet nutritionally balanced diet works incredibly well in a broad range of animals, increasing longevity and prolonging good health." [1]

Lean Dogs Live Longer. The data is clear with worms, flies, mice, rats, monkeys, dogs and humans. Reducing calorie consumption extends the animal's life. A 2003 study of more than 900,000 adults for 16 years showed that overweight and obese people had death rates from all cancers combined that were 52% higher for men and 62% higher for women than the rates in men and women of normal weight.[2] The same is probably true for dogs.

Barry Sears, the force behind The Zone Diet, sums up the studies on humans: "calorie restriction is the only proven way to reverse the aging process.... First, by reducing calorie intake (especially high-density carbohydrate foods such as starches, grains, bread and pasta), you will automatically reduce insulin levels...." He lists increased life span, learning ability, improved immune function, kidney function and female fertility as some of the changes occurring in humans that restrict their caloric intake.[3]

A recently completed 14-year Ralston Purina study with dogs concluded that a 25% reduction in food intake significantly increased the lifespan of dogs. At the midpoint of that study, the results were clear. Dogs free-fed (a dry dog food) started developing arthritis at the age of two. Dogs kept lean did not begin to develop arthritic changes until they were eight or nine. At the conclusion of the study, results were just as dramatic: lean dogs died two years later and the muscle wasting associated with old age was delayed two years.[4]

These studies show that undernutrition, not malnutrition, dramatically extends life span. We believe one reason undernutrition increases life span is that the more food we eat, the more metabolic (conversion of food energy to vital processes and activities) waste products we produce. Some of the waste products are free oxygen, called free radicals, which damages cells. The fewer calories we consume, the fewer free radicals we produce. Hence the need to consume low-calorie, high-antioxidant content foods like vegetables and high quality proteins from fresh meats. These foods provide the most nutrition for the least amount of calories, certainly when compared to feeding grains or potatoes, which probably provide the least amount of nutrition per calorie.

More than half the dogs we meet are overweight. Studies by petfood companies estimate 25 to 50% of dogs are overweight.[5] Sometimes it is not easy to get them to lose weight. Some dogs, like some people, just like to eat and eat and eat. This may be due to a malnutrition problem in the womb.[6] It may be due to the metabolic effect of a high-grain diet. Nevertheless, it is important that these dogs lose weight.

IT'S NEVER TOO LATE TO GET THE BENEFITS
OF BEING LEAN

Even if your dog is heavy now, switching to a lower-calorie and reduced carbohydrate diet may help her live longer. Studies with fruit flies suggest that switching to a restricted diet at any age can yield the benefit of increased longevity.[7] Studies with mice conducted by the National Institute of Aging (NIA) suggest that fasting helps increases lifespan. The NIA studies suggest that reduced meal frequency (eating every other day) can produce beneficial health effects even if the animals gorged when they eat. Meal-skipping diets can stimulate brain cells to produce a protein that promotes the survival and growth of new cells.[8]

Meal skipping may help your Spot live longer, but the quality of his life, and your life, may not improve. A hungry dog is not necessarily a happy dog. And, as Steve learned when he asked BeeBop, Zach's granddaughter, to fast, a hungry dog can be a big pest!

Tiny dogs and puppies are not good candidates for long fasts: they need to eat more frequently. Serious health problems like hypoglycemia and seizures have been seen as a result of fasting in these two groups. Research your breed and check with your veterinarian to be sure that your dog will benefit from fasting.

HOW MUCH FOOD DOES A DOG NEED?

This is a question we're asked everyday. Our answer: It depends. Let's take an extreme example, a shorthaired Chihuahua who lives in Minneapolis, MN.

Food is energy. The dog needs energy for two general purposes; to fuel all metabolic needs (to feed the body), and to overcome heat loss, to keep the body warm. The dog's normal temperature is 101.5°F. At 98.6, their cells do not function properly.[9] The Chihuahua, a warm weather dog, has a lot of surface area through which he can lose heat, compared to the volume or the mass of the dog. A St. Bernard, on the other hand, has a much smaller surface area/mass ratio and therefore will retain more heat. If the Chihuahua goes outside in the winter, he'll need to consume a lot of food in order to stay warm. Depending upon how long he stays outside, he may need three times more food in the winter than he does in the summer.

The quantity to feed your particular dog varies widely regardless of the food or the manufacturer's instructions. Each body is different. Feed your dog the amount of food that keeps her lean. Dogs that are overweight on seemingly tiny portions of dry food may be having trouble with metabolizing it, and therefore may have a malnutrition or metabolism problem. This does not necessarily indicate a problem with the dog; this dog may not be able to use a highly processed, grain-based food in a bag without harm to her body. The food is the culprit. These dogs need at least some fresh food.

If you're not sure how much to feed your dog, err on the "too little" side. Some pet food companies may recommend feeding too much in their feeding guidelines. A January 2003 article in *Petfood Industry* stated: "studies indicate NRC (National Research Council) guidelines are too high."[10] Many pet food companies base their feeding guideline on NRC data.

BEWARE OF LARGE BISCUITS

We all love to treat our dogs. Sometimes we treat our dogs to reward them for doing what they are told, but most of the time we give them treats because we love the interaction with our dogs. Dogs show their happiness when we give them treats, and that gives us pleasure. The treats we give our dogs are often one of the highlights of the dog's daily life. It's important to them, and it's important to us. But unless we give our dogs the right treats, we may be shortening their lives.

Treats are often a major source of calories. A large biscuit or green treat may have more than 100 kilocalories. A typical adult 40 pound dog needs only about 1,000 kilocalories per day. Therefore one extra biscuit a day can cause a dog to gain a pound a month, or 12 pounds per year. The grain and gluten content of these foods can add considerably to the carbohydrate level of the diet, and the stress placed upon the digestive system.

The size of the treat is not important to dogs (though taste certainly is!), it's the interaction and play with their humans that is important. We therefore recommend tiny treats. (Charlee Bear® Dog Treats have only 2.5 kilocalories per treat.) Remember that tiny treats can include small pieces of meat, bananas, cheese, lettuce, a blueberry—whatever comes to light when you open the refrigerator; fresh food!

CHAPTER 17
Exercise Often When the Conditions are Right

> *"A dog that rarely runs is like*
> *a Porsche that rarely goes faster than 10 mph."*
> *—Steve & Zach, 1993*

Steve and Zach met thousands of purebred and mixed breed dogs and did not see hybrid vigor, the extra vigor and good health expected in mixed-breed dogs. (See Appendix A, The Riddle of Missing Hybrid Vigor). Lack of proper nutrition was not the only reason. Just as with humans, lack of quality exercise is a major problem with dogs, especially large dogs. Small dogs fare a little better: if they are inclined to action, they can get quite a workout racing around inside.

OUR DOG'S ANCESTORS GOT PLENTY OF EXERCISE

Thinking from an evolutionary perspective, our dog's ancestors got plenty of exercise, of many different types. Several times throughout the day, the dog probably had to sprint short distances fast, turn and cut quickly (chasing mice for instance); and, at times, run or walk long distances. And then, of course, sleep.

Hard exercise—rigorous exercise, with the dog panting, is necessary for dogs to be at their best (except in hot weather). Indeed, physical changes occur in the dog's blood and muscles after hard exercise.[1] We all think fitness is important. That importance goes far beyond the superficial. Brains and guts are intimately connected, and neither work well without some vigorous exercise.

EXERCISE MAKES EVERYTHING WORK

Let's examine this a little more closely, from a holistic point-of-view. The more we move, the more our brains are exercised. As this happens, brain cells become stronger and healthier. The brain fires excitatory messages to the brain stem, which is the home of the vital centers of the body. Cells in the brain stem fire to control all autonomic (automatic) centers; heart, digestion, and breathing.

One area of the brain stem sends messages via the vagus nerves to control gut function, including motility (peristalsis, the process by which feces move along the intestines on their way out), secretion of enzymes, acids, and other digestive juices that digest food into the smaller sub-units which make food usable for the body. The better the brain works, the better the guts work. Bowels move faster and better with exercise than without. The toxins being excreted have less chance of being reabsorbed by the body when they are disposed of promptly. We can feed our dogs and cats and ourselves the best food in the world—and if the brain is not functioning at a high level, digestion will be impaired. That great food will not be digested well enough to be fully useful to the body. Much undigested food will be excreted.

Far beyond the waste of money if food is excreted unused, if the digestive system is not working properly, undigested food in the gut becomes directly harmful. Many components of the immune system are made in the gut, but not if it's not working well. Maldigested and inappropriate food can be irritating to the body in many ways, setting the stage for Dysbiosis, Leaky Gut Syndrome, Irritable Bowel Disease and Irritable Bowel Syndrome.

To strengthen the brain with exercise, we must push the system. It will always default to what it's used to, and it will go no further. Steady, progressive exercise, increasing slowly, conditions the heart and cardiac system, oxygenating blood cells and exchanging oxygen. Oxygen is the fuel for the cells of the nervous system, increasing the frequency of firing and allowing more information to be sent to all the cells of the body, improving heart and lung function, which sends better information back to the brain.

Simply, exercise provides more oxygen to the brain—which makes healthier brain cells to send information to every cell in the body. A reverse process is often seen: little exercise results in a sluggish brain, which makes us feel fatigued and less inclined to exercise, a condition that is self-perpetuating.

LEARN SENSIBLE PRECAUTIONS AND LIMITATIONS

Be cautious when exercising puppies. Most puppies should not go for long runs. Consult a knowledgeable veterinarian, or an expert either in your breed or in dog sports about exercising your dog. Be aware of your dog's general condition when exercising, and start slowly. For example, while regular exercise keeps older dogs fit and healthy much longer than those who are not exercised, you need to understand your dog's state of health to avoid injury. And consider your own fitness level as well!

Reduce exercise in hot weather, except for swimming, especially for large dogs. Dogs have much more trouble getting rid of excess heat than humans do. When humans exercise, we eliminate the heat build-up mostly by sweating all over our bodies. Dogs can only sweat through their pads. They pant to cool their heads and brains and the core of the body. They also radiate heat to help cool the body. (If the weather is hot, radiative cooling plays a minor role). Learn the basics symptoms of heat stress and know what to do about them, in case you get into a situation where it is clear that your dog is in trouble.

Generally speaking, big dog breeds developed in cold climates, and small, thin dog breeds developed in warm climates. The larger the dog, the harder it is for the dog to eliminate excess heat. A large, hairy dog may have difficulty surviving on its own in a hot climate. On the other hand, that dog will be able to retain heat and stay warm in cold climates. The insulation of the coat of a husky, for example, provides more insulation per inch than does down, and as much as fine wool.

PART FOUR
Conclusion

Eat good quality foods, including lots of vegetables. Get plenty of exercise, avoid toxins....

What works to help extend our human lives works just as well for our dogs. If we act on that advice, we will all live longer, healthier lives. Our dog's lives are too short as it is. Let's keep them around as long as we can.

Popeye, 11 weeks

The pea soup fog rolled in on the coast of Maine. Everything got wet. The computer stopped working, and newspapers became limp like noodles. The fog stayed for weeks. In my kitchen I kept Zach's dry dog food. I'd buy a 40-pound bag of a premium brand food and would use it up in a month. I'd open the bag, scoop the food, roll the bag back up, and then forget about the food until the next meal.

A mold spore, always in the air, landed in the bag before I closed it. The food has absorbed the moisture in the air. A little mold grew, I didn't see it, and Zach didn't taste it. The food had no cancer-fighting properties, it was inappropriate food for dogs to start with… and years later Zach died of cancer.

I have learned a lot since then. BeeBop, Zach's granddaughter, eats a much better diet than Zach did. She eats a variety of fresh foods, and almost never any dry dog food. She is now a two year old, a bright, communicative, healthy "teddy bear." Popeye, Zach's great-grandson, is just a pup. Both dogs show every sign of having hybrid vigor and I expect them to live long, healthy lives.

We all want our Spots to live long, healthy lives. We hope you now have more knowledge about how to improve the odds that yours will.

Thank you for letting us share our knowledge with you.

APPENDIX A
A Closer Look at the Costs of Dog Food

In this section, we present the cost structure of a typical premium dog food sold in a pet food store. First, we examine the mark-ups along the distribution channel.

If you pay $20.00 for a 20-pound bag of dog food, here's where the money goes.

Table A-1: Cost Structure with Pet Food Grade Chicken		
	per pound	*per 20lb bag*
You pay	**$1.00**	**$20.00**
Retailer's margin	25%	25%
Retailer pays	$0.75	$15.00
Distributor's margin	22%	22%
Distributor pays	$0.59	$11.70
Freight to distributor	$0.06	$1.20
Manufacturer sales price	$0.53	$10.50
Manufacture margin	45%	45%
Manufacturer cost	$0.29	$5.78
Bag, processing, pallet, etc.	$0.10	$1.90
Ingredient cost	**$0.19**	**$3.88**

A manufacturer sells its products to a distributor. The distributor warehouses and delivers the product to retailers. Margin is the percentage profit on the sale price. For example, if a retailer sells a product for $1.00 and makes 35¢, their margin is 35%. Retailers buy the food from distributors and sell the food to the public. In the authors' opinions, the distributor has the toughest job in the industry: high overhead, trucks breaking down, difficult manufacturers. Most pet food manufacturers strive for gross margins of 40 to 50%. Selling dog food, especially high end dry foods and raw diets, requires a lot of time and effort to educate people. Dog food distributed through mass merchandisers may have lower margins for the entire distribution channel than foods sold through pet food stores.

This analysis is based upon an average ingredient price of 19 cents per pound, very similar to the premium food presented in Chapter 8. Let's examine what happens if this food uses human-edible chicken, rather than pet food quality. Here is the recipe for the food:

Table A-2: Ingredient Cost, Pet Food Grade Chicken		
Ingredient	*% in recipe*	*Cost/lb.*
CHICKEN MEAL	30%	$0.26
CRACKED BARLEY	27%	$0.13
BREWERS RICE	26%	$0.09
POULTRY FAT	10%	$0.23
DIGEST	3%	$0.47
TOMATO POMACE	2%	$0.09
POTASSIUM CHLORIDE	0.5%	$0.10
SALT	0.25%	$0.03
VITAMIN MIX	0.10%	$4.50
MINERAL MIX	0.10%	$0.93
YEAST	0.10%	$1.90
CHOLINE CHLORIDE	0.15%	$0.48
NAT PRESERVATIVES	0.04%	$18.36

The manufacturer is using a chicken meal. Since real chicken is about 70% moisture, it takes 3.3 pounds of chicken to make one pound of chicken meal. Let's assume that a large volume manufacturer can buy mechanically deboned chicken (MDM—the same type used in corn dogs and less expensive hot dogs) for 35¢ per pound. That means that one pound of human-edible chicken meal will cost at least $1.17 per pound, not including the cost of drying and packaging. Plugging $1.17 per pound chicken into the recipe, we have increased the average ingredient cost from 19¢ to 51¢ per pound.

Table A-3: Ingredient Cost, Human-edible Chicken		
Ingredient	*% in recipe*	*Cost / lb.*
CHICKEN MEAL	30%	$1.17
CRACKED BARLEY	27%	$0.13
BREWERS RICE	26%	$0.09
POULTRY FAT	10%	$0.23
DIGEST	3%	$0.47
TOMATO POMACE	2%	$0.09
POTASSIUM CHLORIDE	0.5%	$0.10
SALT	0.25%	$0.03
VITAMIN MIX	0.10%	$4.50
MINERAL MIX	0.10%	$0.93
YEAST	0.10%	$1.90
CHOLINE CHLORIDE	0.15%	$0.48
NAT PRESERVATIVES	0.04%	$18.36

Now, let's go back and determine how much this food will retail for. The only change we made is switching from pet food grade chicken to human grade chicken. This change doubles the cost of the dog food, from about $1.00 per pound to almost $2.00 per pound.

Table A-4: Cost Structure, Human-edible Chicken

	per pound	*per 20 bag*
You pay	**$1.99**	**$39.78**
Retailer's margin	25%	25%
Retailer pays	$1.49	$29.84
Distributor's margin	22%	22%
Distributor pays	$1.16	$23.27
Freight to distributor	$0.06	$1.20
Manufacturer sales price	$1.10	$22.07
Manufacture margin	45%	45%
Manufacturer cost	$0.61	$12.14
Bag, processing, pallet, etc.	$0.10	$2.00
Ingredient cost	**$0.51**	**$10.14**

There are no great secrets to making dry dog food. Most manufacturers have similar costs. If you find foods advertised as having "organic" or "human-edible" ingredients, and you're not paying a lot more for them than typical premium dry foods, question the manufacturer closely.

"Meat First" Games Dog Food Manufacturers Play. In the 1980s, some dog food manufacturers heavily promoted the "meat first" position in the ingredient panel. Ingredients are listed in order by weight. If two or more ingredients are used in the same amounts, the manufacturer can choose the order in which to list the ingredients. "Meat first" became a buzz word, and any new premium dog food had to list the meat first, otherwise it looked like it contained less meat, and would not sell.

Some lamb and rice dog food manufacturers are especially good at this game. They may divide the rice into different types of rice (ground rice, rice flour, and rice bran), in order to list the lamb first. Here is the ingredient panel of a popular lamb and rice.

How Much Lamb, How Much Rice?

Lamb meal, Ground Rice, Rice Flour, Rice Bran, Sunflower Oil, Poultry Fat, Natural Flavors, Rice Gluten, Dried Egg Product, Dried Beet Pulp, Potassium Chloride, L-Lysine, Dried Kelp, Salt, Choline Chloride, Zinc Sulfate, Vitamin E Supplement, Taurine, Ferrous Sulfate, Ascorbic Acid, Biotin, Copper Proteinate, Niacin, Manganous Oxide, Calcium Pantothenate, Vitamin B12, Riboflavin, Vitamin A...

Steve had to play the game as well, with his Charlee Bear Dog Food. For example, in Charlee Bear's chicken, rice and egg variety, the first three ingredients in the ingredient panel (listed by weight) for a 5,000 pound batch were: 900 lbs chicken meal, 850 lbs ground brown rice, and 850 lbs ground wheat. Almost twice as much grain as meat, but the meat was listed first.

If you have several large dogs, you may find the cost of a total fresh food diet to be prohibitive. There are also a few dogs in our experience who seem to need a portion of their diet to be grain-based, often hard working dogs like pointer and field dogs. There are ever-increasing choices in the dry food segment of the pet food industry, and choosing a food can be a very confusing and frustrating experience,

The current fashions in pet food mirror those in the human food sector. Advertising tells the consumer that what they will get in dry-food-in-a-bag is—a fresh food diet! Label reading has become a skill requiring great sophistication and subtlety. For example, a major food company has put out a food with beautiful pictures of vegetables and fruit on the bag and—no fruit or vegetables in the bag.

DIETS FOR SPECIFIC LIFE STAGES AND CONDITIONS

Senior and diet foods are, in our opinion, to be avoided.

Senior dogs need better quality protein and fat, and less carbo-hydrate. The studies which led to the "less protein might avoid kidney damage" thinking did not in fact say that less protein should be fed. They said that better quality protein was needed when dogs were showing signs of kidney damage; real food was needed. The current research on this topic is readily available

Dogs who need to lose weight need better quality protein and fat, and less carbohydrate. These dogs are in need of at least some por-tion of their diet as fresh food. If they get half of their food as a fresh diet, it will reduce the carbohydrate level and make it much easier for them to lose weight. We have heard of some people using this idea but still using "lite" dry food. This does not make sense once you think it through: the "lite" food is very high in carbohydrate. If you must, use a regular adult formula and at least half fresh food.

Puppy, performance, and adult foods often prove to be very little different when labels are closely scrutinized. We feel that for most purposes, an adult formula is the best choice. Feed your dog the amount needed to keep him lean but not underweight.

YOUR CHOICES ARE—

The Bottom Level. Mass-merchandiser brands. If you're paying 25 cents a pound for dog food ($10 for 40-pound bag), the raw ingredients probably cost the manufacturer 5 to 8 cents per pound. You get what you pay for. These foods are made of carbohydrate fractions and byproducts, with chemical preservatives, flavor enhancers, and colors designed to make the foods attractive to humans. These companies put a great deal of money into research in two areas: getting the buyer's attention and getting the animal to eat something they would otherwise refuse. Flavor ("palatability") enhancers are made from cheap fats and animal digests which make the food smell more—and better to the dog or cat. Grains in these foods, the major ingredient by weight, are more likely to be contaminated with mycotoxins when they are bought. Meat proteins are the cheapest possible sources available, and it's likely that the crude protein listed on the labels of these foods includes a substantial amount from grain sources. Fats in these foods are often the waste rendered from restaurant grease, etc, and are damaged by the original cooking.

In the Middle Third. The middle group of commercial pet foods are the foods which make an attempt to preserve their foods in less toxic ways—or at least in less visibly toxic ways. The meats are more likely to be single-source meats (chicken meal instead of meat meal), and more whole grains are included. Preservatives like ethoxyquin and BHA and BHT are used less, or at least they are not added, though they may be present. Fats, too, are of better quality. Single source fats and vegetable oils are often used. People often see improvement in their pet's coats, in allergy symptoms, and in gut problems when they switch up to this level of food, and for many people this is the first step in looking for better options.

The Best Dry Foods. These products are made from higher quality ingredients and are often packaged in high barrier bags. Even with these foods, the manufacturers' ingredient cost is in 25 to 35 cents per pound range. High-barrier bags keep out the oxygen and moisture that can migrate through most traditional dog food bags. Oxygen makes the fats go rancid and reduces nutrition; moisture promotes fungal growth. Because these foods are preserved minimally for the most part, it is critically important to keep them in good condition. Freezing in an airtight package probably is the best overall strategy: fats will be protected, and molds will not be given an environment that encourages their growth.

Is it Fresh? Shoppers need to consider freshness and storage conditions. Food is labeled with a "best used by" date, but quality can be negatively impacted by heat and humidity in storage both by the distributor and the retailer. Be especially careful during the summer months. Two months in a hot Texas warehouse can severely damage nutrition, and increase the likelihood of mold and rancidity.

Food that smells rancid, or looks different that what you are familiar with (dusty/moldy) should not be fed. Food that an animal previously was enthusiastic about which is suddenly refused could have to do with a sick dog—or a contaminated food. It doesn't hurt for the human to know how it should smell—smell the food! Train your nose to know what good fresh food smells like. Airtight, cold storage will protect food the best.

Variety is Important. When you have found some foods that meet your criteria, choose a few that your dog does well on and rotate them. Rotating 3 choices on a daily basis (NOT mixing them together) will ask your dog's body for slightly different enzymes and digestive activity every day, giving these systems a better workout. In addition, the ingredients from different brands and different varieties of food give your dog different minerals and raw material sources, and a better chance to provide the wide range of vitamins and minerals desired.

Buying 3 small bags will cost a little more, but it will give you the variety and quality control that's so important. If you find this suggestion cumbersome, try buying different foods each time you buy, after you have discovered a few foods your dog does well on. No one food is right for all dogs or is right for any dog all the time.

The idea of variety may still seem to be a strange one, and there are some dogs who will have difficulty initially with any diet change. These are the dogs who are in the most need of a fresh food diet. If you have one of those dogs, we strongly urge you to consider going to a full-time fresh food diet. It may take a while to switch your dog over, but there is a much better chance of actually solving the problem if fresh food is what the dog eats.

Steve's Hypothesis: The Riddle of Missing Hybrid Vigor

> *"Hybrid vigor is an increase in performance of crossbred*
> *or hybrid animals over that of purebreds,*
> *most noticeably in traits like fertility and survivability."* [1]

Hybrid vigor was well documented in the past, but now appears to be missing or significantly diminished.

I learned about hybrid vigor through my efforts to develop Charlee Bear® Dogs. I first suspected it was missing when I didn't see it in my own breeding program or in thousands of mixed-breed dogs I met throughout the country promoting my dog treats. When I read in a comprehensive textbook on canine diseases that hybrids have just as many diseases, if not more, than pure-breds,[2] I knew something was wrong. What happened to hybrid vigor?

The fact that hybrid vigor is missing is strong evidence that many of the health problems of dogs are caused by environmental factors—inappropriate diets, exposure to toxins, and lack of exercise—and not genetic factors. The good news is that this means many of the problems are preventable.

In this section we're going to look at what hybrid vigor is and why, I believe, it is missing. First, we'll look at how dogs evolved and their natural vigor.

FROM WOLVES TO DOGS WHO ASK PEOPLE FOR HELP

The dog has been a very successful species, with hundreds of millions of dogs sharing all parts of the world with humans. While wolves and many large predators are endangered, dogs have flourished. Until very recently, perhaps the last hundred years, almost all dogs survived on their own. For the most part they found their own food, often at the village garbage dump. Dogs thrived because they are a vigorous, resourceful species. Any dog not vigorous, such as a dog with poor hips who couldn't run well, would probably not survive and would certainly not reproduce.

As dogs evolved from wolves around the human garbage dump, the vigorous wolf dogs who least offended humans (the tamer ones) had the best chance to survive and reproduce. As the dog continued to live closer to humans, those dogs which had the best ability to communicate with humans were most successful and passed on their genes to the next generation.[3] The better the dog understood humans, the better its chances of surviving and reproducing.

Dogs understand people better than probably any other species, including wolves and apes. Even dogs raised in the wild are better at communicating with humans than are wolves raised by humans.[4] Unlike the wolf, the dog has learned to gaze at the human face, to communicate with humans with eye/face contact, and even to ask humans for help.[5] The dog looks at our face and often understands what we want, and even what we're planning to do. We only have to think about going for a walk, and the dog is up, yawning, telling us "I'm ready, let's go."

FROM VILLAGE DOG TO PUREBRED

As humans developed more specialized tasks and dogs gradually became tamer, people started developing dog breeds to meet their specific needs. For example, Herr Louis Doberman, a tax collector in the mid-1800s, needed a dog who would protect him and help convince people to pay their taxes. Using at least six different breeds, he developed a very vigorous dog, the Doberman Pinscher. Lord

Tweedmouth, also in the 19th century, used five or more breeds to develop a vigorous hunting dog, the Golden Retriever.[6]

Today, these once vigorous dogs, like almost all purebreds, are often bred primarily to meet physical conformation standards. Outcrossing to other breeds is not allowed. Vigor often suffers. These breeds, like most dog breeds, were established from a small number of founders and now have a closed gene pool. This means that inbreeding is essential to continue the breed.

Inbreeding, though, increases the dogs' susceptibility to pathogens by bringing together rare recessive genes. One would think that the health of these dogs could benefit from outcrossing, adding "hybrid vigor." Hybrids historically have been much less sensitive to individual genetic mutations than purebred dogs because they had greater genetic variation.

IN SEARCH OF HYBRID VIGOR: CHARLEE BEAR® DOGS

In 1983, after a year-long search in shelters throughout the San Francisco Bay area for an adult medium-sized, non-shedding dog,[7] I found a dog I called Charlee. Charlee was a mixed breed dog of unknown background. In order to adopt him from the humane society, I had him neutered.

He was a wonderful companion. He was happy just to be with me (and me with him). He loved to touch and be touched. He seemed to understand me. I took him many places; he was welcome almost everywhere. One day, someone asked me, "He's just like a teddy bear. Where do I get a dog like him?" That question started me on a long, fulfilling journey.

My partner, Chris Gelalich, and I decided to use him as a prototype to develop a special type of mixed breed dog we named Charlee Bear® Dogs. In a sense, we wanted to continue on the evolutionary path of dogs and select our Charlee Bear Dogs for their ability to communicate with humans, to give and receive love, and to touch and be touched. We call these "teddy-bear traits."

As I researched the genetics of dogs, and dog breeding, I read many nineteenth and early twentieth century studies that discussed mixed breeds. Long term studies conducted from the 1880s to the early 1950s documented hybrid vigor in mixed breed dogs. Hybrid vigor was shown to exist in dogs in long-term studies by Dr. Leon Whitney, *How to Breed Dogs*, 1971; Dr. Charles Stockard, *The Genetic and Endocrine Basis for Differences in Form and Behavior*, 1941; and Scott and Fuller's classic study, *Genetics and the Social Behavior of the Dog*, 1965.

Dr. Leon Whitney bred more than 12,000 puppies in his kennels over four decades. He called hybrid vigor "the increased vigor which usually results from hybridizing."[8]

Scott and Fuller, based upon 20 years of research, stated, "The increased body size of the F1 can be attributed to hybrid vigor, and the F2's are in turn affected by this same hybrid vigor in that their F1 mothers had unusually abundant milk supplies and gave them excellent care."[9] (F1 dogs are the first generation mix, F2 are the second generation).

A 1946 book on how to breed dogs states "The crossing to two distinct and unrelated breeds of dogs may produce mongrels of great stamina in the first generation."[10]

Please note that all these studies were conducted before the introduction of extruded foods (1957).

From my studies, I expected mixed breeds to be healthier, with fewer allergy and arthritis problems. I certainly did not expect to find hip problems. How wrong I was.

HOW I LEARNED HYBRID VIGOR WAS MISSING

I Didn't Find Hybrid Vigor in My Breeding Program. I searched for many years to find Garbo and Bogart, the foundation dogs for

Charlee Bear Dogs. When they were two years old they passed their health and personality tests, and in March 1990 we had our first litter. I had originally planned on keeping a girl, but one male puppy was special: the golden-collared puppy, later named Zach. He grew up to be everything I wanted in a dog.

I expected all my first generation Charlee Bears to have excellent health, as well as "teddy-bear" like dispositions. I was only half right. All my dogs were lovers, but they were not as healthy as I expected.

Maggie, Zach's sister, had allergy problems that started when she was just 8 months old. Her guardians did almost everything right; they used no lawn chemicals, no toxic household cleaners. They were careful with everything. So, what was wrong?

Confusing me even more was the fact that one of our first generation Charlee Bear Dogs had worse hips than either of their parents. Our foundation dogs passed their hip tests (testing for hip dysplasia). How could one of their progeny, a first generation mixed breed, fail his hip test? Where was the hybrid vigor?

Zach and I Met 5000 Dogs and Didn't Find Hybrid Vigor. As we've seen, "teddy bear traits" have a genetic basis. The better the dog understood and interacted with humans, the better the chance of surviving and passing on its genes. Certain breeds of dogs, and certain lines of those breeds, are tamer and less aggressive to humans than other breeds. But, for the most part, teddy-bear traits are not born; they are made.

Dogs evolved from wolves because they found that being near humans had more rewards (easier food supply) than living in the wild. In a sense, dogs became dogs because of the positive reinforcement from being around humans. Today, positive reinforcement training techniques, including the judicious use of food rewards, in my opinion, are the best way to train most dogs, (and the only way to train a Charlee Bear Dog).

At a Wendy Volhard dog training camp, I noticed that people were using hot dogs, cheese, and broken biscuits for rewards for their dogs. These rewards left stains or crumbs in people's pockets. I saw a need for a "Pocket Perfect" low calorie dog "training" treat.

In 1992, with Zach, Ava Olsen, some excellent food scientists, bakers and dog trainers, I developed Charlee Bear® Dog Treats. This was my first foray in the dog food industry. Dog trainers loved them and the product became, and still is, a big success. You can find them at Petco, Trader Joe's, Petsmart, and in thousands of pet food stores nationwide.

Zach was our businessdog. He is on the label of Charlee Bear® Dog Treats with me. He loved business and almost always knew what was expected of him. He was especially sweet to buyers! He and I went to about 200 grand openings of Petco and Petsmart stores throughout the nation. We spent months on the road together. This was at a time when these superstore chains were opening stores almost every weekend. We met thousands of people and their dogs. I asked them a lot of questions about the health of their dogs.

I expected to see problems with purebreds, but not to the extent that I did. What totally shocked me was finding the same problems in mixed breed dogs. We saw allergies, arthritis, hip dysplasia, cancer, eye problems, skin problems, and dental problems. So, where was the hybrid vigor that Whitney, Stockard, and Scott and Fuller documented?

How could dogs have survived on their own for 14,000 years with these diseases? Wild dogs with these diseases would produce fewer progeny than fit dogs. Their lines would die out. These problems cannot just be genetic. I concluded there must be environmental reasons for diseases in dogs.

MY SEARCH FOR THE ANSWERS TO THE RIDDLE

From Texas to California to Georgia, Zach and I continued to meet thousands of people and their dogs. My questions became more specific. How much exercise did she get? What food do you feed her? Why? I asked lots of questions, and since most people love to talk about their dogs, I got lots of data.

I learned quickly that dogs were not getting the right type of exercise. Especially for the 90% of the Labradors we met that were overweight! I remember well a heavy, middle-aged woman at a pet store grand opening in Dallas, TX. She had a very fat 18-month old Black Labrador. He looked sad. I asked her about his exercise. Her indignant response was classic: "He gets plenty of exercise. I walk him twice a day!"

It was the hundreds of similar stories from purebred and mixed-breed dog guardians about lamb and rice diets that began to open up my mind about canine nutrition. I realized the now almost folklore adage "never change your dog's diet" is a major part of the problem.

The Lamb and Rice Phase. "He had bad allergies. Then I switched him to Lamb and Rice. His coat got better, he smelled better. But then a year later, he started losing his hair again... now I have him on fish and potato but he's getting heavy."

These stories made me realize that the allergy problem had to have a nutritional cause, not a genetic one. We all know that people need to eat a variety of foods, but so do dogs.

I decided to develop a variety-based dry dog food, so that the dog would eat a chicken based food one day, beef the next, turkey the next. Charlee Bear Dog Treats were selling well at Petsmart, and Petsmart liked the Charlee Bear brand. I discussed my concept about a variety-based dry dog food with Dr. Mark Finke, a bright canine nutritionist then at Petsmart. He thought the idea had merit, had me research the concept with leading canine nutritionists, and visit many dog food plants to determine where best to manufacture the food.

Charlee Bear® Variety-based Dog Food. I visited many dog food plants, and learned first hand how food was made. If you ever have a chance to visit a dog food plant, look for the ingredients. Most likely, they'll all be in bags. Only a few manufacturers have the freezer and refrigerator space needed to store fresh foods.

I fed my dogs many different dry and canned foods, including all the "best brands." I worked closely with the late Ross Becker, the founder of *Good Dog Magazine*, to compare results. Ross probably tested more dog foods than anybody. I never noticed much of a change with my dogs. They were used to variety and handled each food well.

Working with some excellent canine nutritionists, I formulated three varieties of high quality kibble. We produced some test batches of the foods. The dogs liked them, and our marketing studies showed that most people accepted the variety concept. Most people seem to understand, intuitively, that variety is good for dogs.

Then Garbo Ate a Raw Diet. The first time I fed a raw diet to my dogs was in September 1996. Two weeks after starting the raw diet, Garbo, Zach's Mom, started running with the younger dogs again. She was 11 years old, and for the last two years she had been walking with me when I went into the woods, instead of running with Zach and the younger dogs. A week later I noticed that the sebaceous cysts she had developed had dramatically shrunk. I sent many of my Charlee Bear Dog families raw diets and they saw similar results. The dogs loved the food, and they thrived.

I was no longer interested in any type of kibble. I decided to develop a variety of easy-to-use raw diets for dogs.

Six years and two generations of Charlee Bear Dogs later, I'm pleased to report that each generation of raw fed dogs gets better and better. My last litter was the healthiest, smartest, most communicative litter I've ever seen. My hybrid dogs are showing hybrid vigor!

Is His Health Problem Genetic, "Womb Effect," or What I Fed Him?

Where do health problems in dogs "originate?" Many people, including veterinarians, often conclude that many canine diseases, including most cancers and Canine Hip Dysplasia, are primarily genetic in origin. This is understandable, especially considering the rapidly increasing awareness—and press—about genes.

Nevertheless, if a dog is born with a health problem, it does not necessarily mean the problem has a genetic origin.

Even if the health problem "runs in the family," i.e. his mother and grandmother had the same problem, it still may not have a genetic component. We'll start this discussion with a look at a serious problem with many pure and mixed breed dogs: Canine Hip Dysplasia (CHD). Hip dysplasia is a malformation of the ball and the socket of the hip joint.

How Can Canine Hip Dysplasia (CHD) Be Genetic? While writing this book, Steve took his dogs to one of the local dog parks. Eugene Oregon is wonderful place for dogs (if they don't mind the rain). There are six dog parks in Eugene, a small city, and, close by, mountains where dogs can run, hike and camp with their humans.

At the dog park, Steve met a 14-month-old mixed breed dog. He looked to be a typical "village dog" about 30 pounds, and had a yellow coat. He had serious hip problems and could barely run. His guardian, who had him since he was a young puppy, said she thought he was from a long line of "mutts." She told Steve that he never ran well, and recently starting limping. The veterinarian diagnosed hip dysplasia and said it was probably a genetic defect. We question how this mixed-breed dog's hip problems can be a genetic issue. Where is the hybrid vigor?

It takes a fit dog to survive and reproduce in the wild. A high percentage of the young from all mammals, except humans and with us only recently, do not survive to reproductive age. It's survival of the fittest. Genetic traits that are unfavorable to an organism's survival or reproduction do not persist in the gene pool for very long. From an evolutionary perspective, there can be no "genes for hip dysplasia." Dogs with malformed hips would not survive in the wild and would not reproduce.[1]

The hybrid dog in the park may have been born with hip problems, but it is unlikely to be a genetic defect. Traits which are concerned with viability—the ability to run—are more likely to exhibit hybrid vigor,[2] and therefore less likely to be genetic.

Given the evidence we see, we believe that malnutrition and exposure to toxins in the womb, are major causes of CHD and canine elbow dysplasia in most pure-bred dogs and probably the vast majority of mixed-breed dogs. No doubt there are many contributing factors, including a moderate degree of heritability in some breeds. Obesity is a risk factor for CHD in all breeds.[3] We believe that feeding pregnant dogs and puppies human-synthesized forms of vitamins and especially trace minerals, instead of natural, organic forms, may be a major contributing factor to CHD (Please see Chapter 7 and the discussion of the different forms of selenium). This is a controversial issue. Some highly respected scientists think CHD is strictly genetic.

Many breeders, including Steve, report significantly reduced CHD problems in the second generation of proper raw fed dogs.

"It Runs In the Family." Just because a disease runs "in the family" does not make it a genetic disease. The disease may be caused by exposure to toxins or poor nutrition in the womb (congenital or "womb effect") and during the first several weeks of life; or it may be caused by exposure to toxins or poor nutrition once we bring young puppies into our homes.

For example, let's say you have three generations of dogs that died from liver cancer at age 8. Grandma, ma, and grandson. Many people may jump to the conclusion "I have liver cancer in my line, it must be a genetic problem." But what if all three dogs drank water from puddles laced with carcinogens from a neighbor's lawn? Or all were exposed to low levels of aflatoxin-contaminated dog foods, and never ate green vegetables? We know that these environmental toxins cause cancer. Sometimes, liver cancer runs in the family because of the environment, not because of genes.[4]

"The Womb Effect." There is a growing body of evidence that inadequate nutrition in early childhood and in the womb increases the risk of a variety of diseases later on,[5] including second generation health problems that may appear to be genetic.

Ellen Shell, in *Hungry Gene, the Science of Fat and the Future of Thin*, discusses the published work and her conversations with Dr. David Barker, one of the leading researchers on the fetal origins of adult diseases.[6] Dr. Barker says that conditions in the womb and early childhood program the way one's kidneys, liver, pancreas, heart and brain develop and how they function later in life. Dr. Parker's "fetal origins" hypothesis proposes that many diseases originate through undernutrition during critical periods of early development. He states:

"The undernourished baby changes its growth, physiology and metabolism. These changes tend to persist through life."[7] Dr. Barker's ideas have spread.

According to the June 14th, 2003 issue of *The Economist*, his

"Fetal Origins of Adult Disease" hypothesis is now the subject of investigation by researchers all over the world. The article summarizes the studies: "Heart disease, obesity and late-onset diabetes frequently seem to trace their origins back to conditions in the womb, or in the first few weeks of infancy. So do cognitive ability, earning power, and even greed and sloth."[8] Dr. Parker also determined that stroke may originate through malnutrition in the womb.[9]

Shell wrote: "Studying populations in China, Finland, and India, Barker and others have found evidence that chronic diseases spawned in the womb can be passed down through generations, almost like a genetic trait. When an overweight mother overproduces insulin, for example, the hormone crosses through the placenta into the fetus. Too much insulin will tax the fetal pancreas, predisposing the child to diabetes, which she may then pass down to her children. Unless something is done to curtail it, this vicious cycle of ill health can continue indefinitely."[10]

Shell and Matt Ridley, in *Nature via Nurture*,[11] discuss the Dutch famine studies. Near the end of World War II, from September 17, 1944 until liberation May 5, 1945, the Germans ordered an embargo on all civilian transport going into Holland. The result was a devastating seven-month famine. Some 40,000 people were fetuses during the famine. Their birth weight and later health are on record. Studies conducted in the 1960s found all the expected effects of undernourished mothers, including a second-generation effect. Ridley explains: "Babies who were in the first six months of gestation during the famine were of normal birth weight, but when they reached adult-hood they themselves gave birth to unusually small babies."[12]

The mother doesn't have the resources to give the fetus the proper nutrition; that child as an adult, therefore, is more likely not to have the resources to give her fetus the proper nutrition.

Raw canine and feline diet proponents often refer to multi-generational studies conducted by Dr. Francis Pottenger.[13] Between the years of 1932 and 1941, Dr. Pottenger conducted feeding experiments to determine the effects of heat-processed food on cats. His study included 900 cats. In one of his experiments, he fed one group of cats a diet of 2/3 raw meat, 1/3 raw milk and cod liver oil. The second group of cats received 2/3 cooked meat, 1/3 raw milk and cod liver oil. He found that kittens born from the cooked meat diet had deficient skeletons, heart problems, infections of the kidneys, testes, ovaries, bladder, and many other problems. When these kittens were bred, producing second generation kittens, the problems were more profound, and symptoms occurred at younger ages. In the third generation, the problems were even worse. (We now know that cooking the meat significantly reduced the amounts of taurine in the diet, causing some of the health problems. Pet food regulators now require additional taurine in cooked cat foods.)

Pottenger found that cats fed a raw diet remained normal. He also found that the line of cats fed the cooked meat diet required approximately four generations of properly fed cats to regenerate to a state of normal health, though improvements in resistance to disease was noted in the second generation.

Conclusion. There is no doubt some dogs, like some people, have a genetic predisposition to certain types of diseases. Good genes are important to the health of our dogs. Beth has been looking for genetically perfect, healthy purebred dogs for decades. Steve has been looking for "good health genes" with his Charlee Bear Dogs.

After years of study, we now believe that conditions in the womb and early life, and what we feed and how we protect our dogs once we get them, are just as important as genes for the long-term health of our dogs.

If you're getting a puppy, make sure the Mom is fed primarily a fresh, raw diet, kept away from toxins, and is in good health. When pregnant, the dog should eat no grain-based foods. We fear that the consumption of even small quantities of mycotoxins from the low-quality grains in dry foods may result in various forms of cancer many years later.

ENDNOTES

INTRODUCTION

1. Milner, John A. "Nonnutritive Components in Foods as Modifiers of the Cancer Process." *Preventive Nutrition: The Comprehensive Guide for Health Professionals,* Second Edition, 2001. 131.
2. London, Cheryl, Veterinary Oncologist. *UC Davis Health Systems Report,* April 19, 2002. http://pulse.ucdavis.edu/scripts/0102/cancerresearch.html
3. *Petfood Industry Electronic Newsletter,* April 1, 2003. Vol. 3, No. 7. Nestle Purina and American Kennel Club news release.

PART TWO: CHAPTER 4

1. Coppinger, Ray and Lorna. *Dogs: A Startling New Understanding of Canine Origin, Behavior, & Evolution.* New York: Scribner, 2001. 59–78.
2. Landry and Van Kruiningen. "Food Habits of Feral Carnivores: A Review of Stomach Content Analysis." *Journal of the American Animal Hospital Association,* November 1979. Vol. 15. 775–781.
3. Savolainen, Zhang, Luo, Lundeberg, Leitner. "Genetic Evidence for an East Asian Origin of Domestic Dog." *Science,* Vol. 298, November 2002. 1610–1613.
4. Clutton-Brock, Juliet. "Origins of the dog: domestication and early history", in *The Domestic Dog, its evolution, behavior and interactions with people,* edited by James Serpell, Cambridge University Press, 1995. 8.
5. Coppinger: 23.
6. Eaton, Boyd, Eaton, Stanley, Konner, Melvin and Shostak, Majorie. "An Evolutionary Perspective Enhances Understanding of Human Nutritional Requirements." *Journal of Nutrition* 1996, 126. 781.
7. Buddington, Randal. "Structure and Functions of the Dog and Cat Intestine." *Proceedings of the 1996 Iams International Nutrition Symposium.* 61–71.

8.   Case, Cary and Hirakawa. *Canine and Feline Nutrition*, Mosby, 1995. 146.
9.   Coppinger: 123–140.

CHAPTER 5

1.   John Hopkins Health. *Allergies*. Time Life Books, 1999. 82.
2.   Ackerman, Lowell. *Skin and Haircoat Problems in Dogs*, Alpine Publications, Loveland, CO 1994. 6.
3.   Innovative Veterinary Diets. *Adverse Reactions to Food: Understanding the Disease, the Diagnosis and its Management*. 1998.
4.   White, Patricia DVM, MS, DACVD. "Update on Canine Food Allergy." presented at Western Veterinary Conference, February 2003. Atlanta Veterinary Skin and Allergy Clinic.
5.   Purina Veterinary Diets. HA, HypoAllergenicTM Canine Formula. VET5301B–0201. 2002.
6.   From personal experience, many conversations with variety feeders, and from the article "Basic Mechanisms: Defining the role of taste and smell in food intake" by Israel Ramirez, published in *Focus on Palatability Proceedings*, published by Petfood Industry, 1995. 11.
7.   Thorne, Chris. "Understanding Pet Response: Behavioral Aspects of Palatability." *Focus on Palatability Proceedings*, 1995. 27.
8.   Council for Agricultural Science and Technology, Ames, Iowa, USA, *Mycotoxins: Risks in Plant, Animal, and Human Systems*, January, 2003. 23.
9.   Lasky, Sun, Kadry, and Hoffman. "Mean Total Arsenic Concentrations in Chicken 1989–2000 and Estimated Exposures for Consumers of Chicken." *Environmental Health Perspectives*, Vol. 112, No. 1, January 2004. 18–21.
10. Mahan, Kathleen and Escott, Sylvia. *Krause's Food, Nutrition & Diet Therapy*, W.B. Saunders Co, 1996. 810.
11. McCay, Clive. *Nutrition of the Dog*, Comstock Publishing Company, 1944. 26.
12. McCay: 30.
13. Schroeder, H.A. "Losses of Vitamins and Trace Minerals Resulting from Processing and Preservation of Foods." *American Journal of Clinical Nutrition* 24 (5), 1971. 562–573.
14. Ghebremeskel, K and M.A. Crawford. "Nutrition and Health in Relation to Food Production and Processing." *Nutritional Health* 9 (4) 1994. 237–253.
15. Coelho, Michael. "How to Ensure Vitamin Stability." *Feed Management*, January 2000, 17.

16. Kimura and Itokaway. "Cooking losses of minerals in foods and its nutritional significance." *Journal of Nutritional Science,* (Tokyo) 1990. 36, Supplement 1S. 25–33.

17. Garrison and Somer. *The Nutrition Desk Reference,* Keats Publishing, 1995. 66–145.

18. Puupponen-Pimia et al. "Blanching and long-term freezing affect various bioactive compounds of vegetables in different ways." *Journal of the Science of Food and Agriculture,* 83 2003. 1389–1402 .

19. Coelho: 17–18.

20. Coelho: 18.

21. Greaves, J., Mann, J. and Haworth J. "Natural Alternatives," *Petfood Industry,* March 2001. 28.

22. *Encyclopedia Britannica,* s.v. "soil" http://www.britannica.com/eb/article?eu=117551 Accessed September 5, 2002.

23. Banwart, George J. *Basic Food Microbiology,* Chapman and Hall, Second Edition, 1989. 166.

24. de Duve, Christian. *Life Evolving,* Oxford University Press, 2002. 11.

25. Bluck, John. NASA News, Ames Research Center, April 3, 2002. From Spring 2002 *Journal of Astrobiology.*

26. Tierno, Philip. *The Secret Life of Germs,* Simon & Schuster 2001. 147.

27. Gershon, Michael. *The Second Brain,* HarperCollins 1998. 147.

28. Gershon: 152.

29. Morgan, K. *Science News,* February 15, 2003.

30. Banwart: 38.

31. Greaves, John. "Reducing Pathogens." The Petfood Forum 2003, Proceedings 380.

32. Strombeck, D. *Home Prepared Dog and Cat Diets, the Healthful Alternative,* Iowa State Press, 1999. 45.

33. Fox, Nicols. *Spoiled* Penguin Books 1998. 155. (From *Proceedings, National Conference on Salmonella,* HEW, 1964.)

34. Stevens, C.E. and Hume, Ian. *Comparative Physiology of the Vertebrate Digestive System,* Second Edition. Cambridge University Press, 1995. 58.

35. Burger, I., Ed. *The Waltham Book of Companion Animal Nutrition,* Pergamon 1995. 26–27.

36. Banta, Clemens, Krinsky, and Sheffy. "Sites of Organic Acid Production and Patterns of Digesta Movement in the Gastrointestinal Tract of Dogs." *Journal*

of Nutrition, Vol. 109, Sept. 1979. 1592.

37. Ragir, Sonia, Rosernberg, Martin, and Tierno. "Gut Morphology and the Avoidance of Carrion among Chimpanzees, Baboons, and Early Hominids." *Journal of Anthropological Review*, 56 (4) 2000.

38. Cannon, W.M. *The Mechanical Factors of Digestion*, New York, 1911. 89 (quoted from McCay: 19.)

39. Dinsmore, J.E., R.J. Jackson and S.D. Smith. 1997. "The protective role of gastric acidity in neonatal bacterial translocation." *J. Pediatr. Surg.* 32:1014–1016. From Alltech's 17th Annual Symposium. 2001.

40. Tierno: 128.

41. Blaxter, Kenneth. *Energy Metabolism in Animals and Man*, Cambridge University Press, 1989. 26.

42. Tierno: 129.

43. Costello, Papasouliotis, Barr, et al. "Determination of solid and liquid phase gastric emptying half times in cats by use of nuclear scintigraphy." *AJVR* Vol. 60, No. 10, December 1999. 1222–1226.

44. Burrows, Kronfeld, Banta & Merritt. "Effects of Fiber on Digestibility and Transit Time in Dogs." *Journal of Nutrition, Vol. 112, No 9*, September 1982. 1731.

45. Stevens: 135; Banta: 1592.

46. Burrows: 1731.

47. Rubenstein, Mark, Haspel, Ben-Ari, Dresnik, Mirelman, and Tadmor. "Antibacterial activity of the pancreatic fluid." *Gastroenterology* April 1985, 88(4). 927–932.

48. Salzman et al. "Gut Defense." *Nature* April 2003. 522.

49. Abbott, Alison. "Gut Reaction." *Nature*, Vol. 427, January 22, 2004. 284–285.

50. Travis, John. "Gut Check." *Science News* Vol. 163, May 31, 2003. 344.

51. Clark, Ton. "Gut Bugs Sequenced. Raecces survey finds new viruses." *Nature*, October 14, 2003.

52. Bourlioux, Koletzko, Guarner, and Braesco. "The intestine and its microflora are partners for the production of the host: report on the Danone Symposium 'The Intelligent Intestine,' held in Paris, June 14, 2002." *American Journal of Clinical Nutrition*, 2003, 78. 675.

53. www.fsis.usda.goc/OA/recalls.

54. From *Science News*, Vol. 155, No. 4, January 23, 1999. 83.

55. Root, Tamis. Food Products Laboratory, Portland, Oregon. September 2002.

56. North Carolina State University Co-operative Extension www.ces.ncsu.edu. "Safe Mycotoxin Levels."Accessed October 2002.

57. "Beyond smallpox." *Scientific American News Scan,* May 2003. 23.

58. Bingham, Phillips, and Bauer. "Potential for dietary protection against the effects of aflatoxins in animals." *Journal of the American Veterinary Medical Association,* Vol. 222, No. 5, March 1, 2003. 591.

59. Money, Nicholas P. "The mysterious world of mushrooms, molds, and mycologists." *Mr. Bloomfield's Orchard,*Oxford University Press, 2002. 75.

60. Pohl, Otto. "Disease Dustup." *Scientific American,* July 2003. 18–20.

61. Banwart: 312.

62. Prescott, Harley, and Klein. *Microbiology, Fourth Edition,* McGraw-Hill, 1999. 910.

63. Council for Agricultural Science and Technology, (CAST) Ames, Iowa. Task Force Report, No. 139. "*Mycotoxin Risks in Plant, Animal, and Human Systems.*" January 2003. 18.

64. The data we've seen from manufacturers of antimicrobials shows that after four days at above 12% moisture mold growth starts.

65. Banwart: 106.

66. Hughes, Graham & Grieb. "Overt Signs of Toxicity to Dogs and Cats of Dietary Deoxynivalenel." *Journal of Animal Sciences,* 1999. 77: 699–700.

67. Bingham et al. 593.

68. Chafee & Hines. "Aflatoxicosis in Dogs." *American Journal of Veterinary Research,* Vol. 30, No. 10, October 1969, 1747–1748. In this 1969 study, four of the dogs tested were given just one dose of aflatoxin; two a high dose, and the other two half a dose. The two with the highest doses died within 26 hours. One of the dogs given a single moderate dose survived. When the dog was euthanized 47 days after infection the authors found a diseased liver and other internal problems. No estimates were made on how long the dog would have lived if it were not euthanized.

69. The CAST report on mycotoxins details the many different types of cancer, affecting all organs in the body, that can result from the long term ingestion of low levels of mycotoxins.

70. Egner et al. "Chlorophyllin intervention reduces aflatoxin-DNA adducts in individuals at high risk for liver cancer." *Proceedings of the National Academy of Sciences USA,* December 4, 2001 Vol. 98, Issue 25, 14601–14606. This study of humans

in China discussed how the symptoms of liver cancer may not appear until 20 years after ingestion of aflatoxin-contaminated grains. Consumption of chlorophyllin delayed the onset of symptoms of liver cancer.

71. Money stated that "The damaging effects of aflatoxin ingestion do not seem to be apparent for many months or years…" 165.

CHAPTER 6

1. Calculated by Steve Brown, 2001, using data from Landry and Van Kruiningen. "Food habits of Feral Carnivores: A Review of Stomach Content Analysis."
2. Innovative Veterinary Diets, "Feline Struvite and Calcium Oxalate Urolithiasis." IVD Innovations.
3. Dr. David Ludwig. Harvard Medical School as quoted in NY Times Magazine, August 7, 2002.
4. Case: 93.
5. Morris, Mark, Lewis, Lone and Hand, Michael. *Small Animal Clinical Nutrition III*, Mark Morris Associates, 1990. 1–11.
6. Burger: 10.
7. McMay: 7.
8. Association of American Feed Control Officals. *Offical Publication*, 2003. 178.
9. Markwell, P.J. *Applied Clinical Mutrition of the Dog and Cat. A guide to Waltham® Veterinary Diets."* 1998. 38.
10. Case: 11.
11. Guptill, Glickman, and Glickman. "Time trends and risk factor for diabetes mellitus in dogs: analysis of veterinary medical data base records (1970–1999)." *Veterinary Journal*, 165(3) 240–247, May 2003.
12. Samaha et al. "A Low-Carbohydrate as Compared with a Low-Fat Diet in Severe Obesity," *The New England Journal of Medicine* Vol. 348: 2047–2081, May 22, 2003; and Foster et al. "A Randomized Trial of Low-Carbohydrate Diet for Obesity." *The New England Journal of Medicine*, Vol. 348: 2082–2090, May 22, 2003.
13. Tierno: 216.
14. Zoran, Debra. "The carnivore connection to nutrition in cats." *JAVMA* Vol. 221, No. 11, December 8, 2002. 1559.
15. Spitze, Wong, Rogers and Fascetti. "Taurine concentrations in animal feed ingredients; cooking influences taurine content." *Journal of Animal Physiology*

and Animal Nutrition, 87(2003). 251–262.

16. Spitze: 260.

17. "Myocardial Failure in Cats Associated with Low Plasma Taurine: A Reversible Cardiomyopathy." *Science,* Vol. 237, 1987. 764–768.

18. Backus, Robert, DVM, PhD. of the University of California, Davis. 2001, reported on AKC website, www.akc.org.

19. Fascetti: 1138.

20. Phillips, Tim. "L-Carnitine. Evidence indicates it may accelerate weight loss and increase lean body mass." *Petfood Industry,* May 2002. 24.

21. Hammel, Kronfeld, Ganjam & Dunlap. "Metabolic responses to exhaustive exercise in racing sled dogs fed diets containing medium, low, or zero carbohydrate," and "Hematological and metabolic responses to training and racing sled dogs containing medium, low, or zero carbohydrate." *The American Journal of Clinical Nutrition* 30, March 1977. 409–418 and 419–430.

22. There are 20 standard amino acids, a rare one (selenocysteine), and a just discovered new amino acid. *Scientific American,* August, 2002. 29.

23. Burger: 13. This is well documented for humans.

24. Morris: 1–15.

25. Bell, Jarold S. "Risk Factors of Canine Bloat." Tufts' Canine and Feline Breeding and Genetics Conference, 2003.

26. Bell, Jarold S. "Risk Factors of Canine Bloat." *AKC* Gazette April 2003. 27.

27. Stevenson AE, et al. "Effect of dietary moisture and sodium content on urine composition and calcium oxalate relative supersaturation in healthy miniature schnauzers and labrador retrievers." *Res Vet Sci* 74 (2): 145–151, April 2003. Lulich et al. "Epidemiology of canine calcium oxalate uroliths. Identifying risk factors." *Vet Clinic North American Small Animal Pract* 29(1): 113–22, January, 1999. Lekcharoensuk et al "Oxalate uroliths in dogs." *American Journal of Veterinary Research* 63(2) 163–169, February, 2002.

28. Steve's Real Food tests at Midwest Laboratories, Omaha, Nebraska July 2002.

29. Ensminger et al. *Foods and Nutrition Encyclopedia, Second Edition.* CRC Press, 1994. 916.

30. *Textbook of Anatomy*

31. Zoran, Debra. "The carnivore connection to nutrition in cats." *JAVMA* Vol. 221, No. 11, December 1, 2002. 1566.

32. Strombeck: 27.

33. Eaton: 1732–1740.

34. Simopoulos, Artemis, and Robinson, Jo. *The Omega Plan,* HarperCollins 1998.

35. Bauer, John. "Fatty acid metabolism in pets." *Feed Management,* March 2000. 13.

36. Cook, Nancy. "Whoa, Pet Food Institute urges changes in the new NRC report." *Petfood Industry,* November 2003. 50–51.

CHAPTER 7

1. Case: 42.

2. Packer, Lester and Colman, Carol. *The Antioxidant Miracle,* John Wiley & Sons, Inc. 1999. 33.

3. Hennekens et al. "Lack of effort of long-term supplementation with beta-carotene on the incidence of malignant neoplams and cardiovascular disease." *New England Journal of Medicine* 334, 1145, 1996; and Omenn et al. "Effects of a combination of beta carotene and vitamin A on lung cancer and cardio-vascular disease." *New England Journal of Medicine,* 334, 1150, 1996. Dr. Packer details many studies that show similar results.

4. Mahan: 811.

5. Cao, Howard, of the Jean Mayer USDA Human Nutrition Research Center, reported in "Can Foods Forestall Aging?" by Judy McBride in *Agricultural Research,* February, 1999.

6. Heart Protection Study Collaborative Group, Redcliffe Infirmary, Oxford, UK. "MRC/BHF Heart Protection Study of antioxidant vitamin supplemen-tation in 20 536 high-risk individuals: a randomized placebo-controlled trial." *The Lancet* Vol. 360, No. 9326, July 06 2002.

7. Borileau, Liao, Kim, Lemeshow, Erdman, and Clinton. "Prostate Carcinogenesis in N-methyl-Nnitrosourea (NMU)—Testosterone-Treated Rats Fed Tomato Powder, Lycopene, or Energy-Restricted Diets." *Journal of the National Cancer Institute,* Vol. 95, No. 21, November 5, 2003. 1578.

8. Lucock, Mark. "Is folic acid the ultimate functional food component of disease prevention?" *British Medical Journal,* Vol. 328, January 24, 2004. 211–214.

9. Waterland and Jirtle. "Transposable Elements: Targets for Early Nutritional Effects on Epigenetic Gene Regulation." *Molecular and Cellular Biology,* Vol. 23, No. 15, August 2003, 5293–5300.

10. U.S. Preventative Services Task Force. "Routine Vitamin Supplementation to Prevent Cancer and Cardiovascular Disease: Recommendations and Rationale." *Annals of Internal Medicine,* Vol. 139 No. 1, July 1, 2003. 51–55.

11. Institute of Medicine of the National Academies, The National Academies

Press. "*Dietary Reference Intakes for Water, Potassium, Sodium, Chloride and Sulfate.*" 2004. 5–12.

12. *The Economist,* Vol. 367, No. 8328, June 14, 2003. 78.

13. Mary E. Reid, Anna J. Duffield-Lillico, Linda Garland, Bruce W. Turnbull, Larry C. Clark, and James R. Marshall. "Selenium Supplementation and Lung Cancer Incidence: An Update of the Nutritional Prevention of Cancer Trial." *Cancer Epidemiology Biomarkers & Prevention.* November 2002, 11.

14. National Toxicology Program, http://ntp-server.niehs.nih.gov/htdocs/STstudies/TOX038.html

15. Hawkes, Alkan, and Oehler. "Absorption, Distribution and Excretion of Selenium from Beef and Rice in Healthy North American Men." *Journal of Nutrition,* November 2003. 3434.

16. Finley, J.W., Ip, C., Lisk, D.J., Davis, C.D., Hintze, K.J. and Whange. "Cancer-protective properties of high-selenium broccoli." *Journal of Agricultural and Food Chemistry,* Vol. 49, No. 5, 2679–2683, 2001.

17. Burk, R.F. & Levander, O.A. "selenium," in Shils, M. et al. *Nutrition in Health and Disease,* Ninth Edition. Baltimore: Williams & Wilkins, 1999. 265–276.

18. Parker, Jay. "Hip Dysplasia in Dogs: Why Seleniuim Deficiency Will Cause It." Unpublished manuscript.

19. Schrauzer, G.N. "Selenomethionine: A Review of its Nutritional Significance, Metabolism and Toxicity." *Journal of Nutrition,* 130, 2000. 1653–1656.

20. Pottenger, Francis. *Pottenger's Cats: A Study in Nutrition.* 1983. Dr. Pottenger compared four generations of cats fed cooked and four generations of cats fed the same diet, except raw. With the cooked diet, Dr. Pottenger found that each generation developed health problems at earlier ages than the preceding generation. The raw fed cats remained healthy. We know that the cooked diets were deficient in taurine and thiamin.

21. University of South Florida Center for Aging and Brain Repair. "Antioxidant-rich diets improve age-related declines in mental function of rats." July15, 2002.

22. Packer: 8.

23. Packer: 118.

24. Brody, Tom. *Nutritional Biochemistry,* Academic Press 1994. 400–406.

25. Berdanier, Carolyn. *Advanced Nutrition,* Micronutrients 1998. 23–27.

26. Talking Point, *The Lancet,* Vol. 361, No. 9374, June 14, 2003. Discussion about article by Vivekananthan et al. "Use of antioxidant vitamins for the

prevention of cardiovascular disease: meta-analysis of randomised trials." *The Lancet*, Vol. 361, No. 9374. 2017–23.

27. Eberhardt, Lee and Liu. "Nutrition: Antioxidant activity of fresh apples." *Nature*, June 22, 2000. 903–904.

28. National Toxicology Program, Technical Report Series No. 409. "Toxicology and Carcinogenesis Studies of Quercetin (CAS No. 117–39–5) in F344 Rats (Feed Studies)." September 1992.

29. Penland, James. "The importance of boron nutrition for brain and psychological Function." USDA, Agricultural Research Service, September 21, 1998.

30. Naghii MR, Samman S. "The role of boron in nutrition and metabolism." *Progressive Food Nutritional Science*. 1993 17: 4. 331–349.

31. Committee on Animal Nutrition Board of Agriculture, National Research Council."The Role of Chromium in Animal Nutrition," National Academy Press, 1997.

32. Kato, Takafumi. Institute of Physical and Chemical Research news release, April 24, 2003, by Reuters.

33. "enzyme" *Encyclopedia Britannica*, http://www.britannica.com/eb/article?eu=33311. Accessed July 11, 2002.

34. Howell, Edward. *Enzyme Nutrition*, Avery Publishing Group, 1985. 73–74.

35. Wysong, Randy. *Lipid Nutrition*, Inquiry Press, 1990. 28.

36. Howell: 12.

37. Ackerman, Lowell. "Effect of an Enzyme Supplement (Prozyme™) on Selected Nutrient Levels in Dogs." *Journal of Veterinary Allergy and Clinical Immunology*, Vol. 2, No. 1, 1993.

38. Newman, Spencer and Epstein, David. "Enzymes: The key to Better Digestion." published in *The Dog Food Book*, Fifth Edition, edited by Ross Becker. 1999.

39. Cichoke, Anthony. *The Complete Book of Enzyme Therapy*, Avery Publishing Company, 1999. 1.

PART THREE

1. Wills & Simpson, editors. *The Waltham Book of Clinical Nutrition of the Dog and Cat*. 1994. 82.

CHAPTER 9

1. Martin, Ann. *Food Pets Die For*, NewSage Press, 1997; and Eckhouse, John, "How Your Dogs and Cats Get Recycled Into Pet Food." San Francisco

Chronicle, February 19, 1990. The pet food industry, partially in response to Martin's book, has worked hard to prevent the use of dead dogs and cats in foods. For more information, contact The Petfood Institute (www. petfoodinstitute.org).

2. Animal Protection Institute. "What's Really in Pet Foods."www.api4-animals.org

3. FDA/Center for Veterinary Medicine Survey. 1998.

4. Canadian Food Inspector Agency, Backgrounder. "Investigation into A Case of Bovine Spomgiform Encephalopathy (BSE) in Alberta." News Release, May 20, 2003.

5. FDA BSE Update. May 2003. www.fda.gov/bbs/topics/NEWS/2003/NEW 0910.html.

6. Sinha, Gustafson, Kulldorff, Wen, Cerhan & Zheng. "2–Amino=1methyl1 –6–phenylimidazo pyridine, a Carcinogen in High-Temperature-Cooked Meat, and Breast Cancer Risk." *Journal of the National Cancer Institute*, Vol. 92, No.16, August 16 2000. 1352–1354.

7. Nerurkar, Le Marchand, Cooney. "Effects of marinating with asian marinades or western barbecue sauce on PhIP and MeIQx formation in barbecued beef." *Nutrition and Cancer*, Vol. 34, Issue 2, 1999. 147.

8. Felton, Salmon, Knize. "Carcinogens formed when Meat is Cooked." Lawrence Livermore National Laboratory, May 30, 2003.

9. Kinze, Salmon, and Felton. "Mutagenic activity and heterocyclic amine carcinogend in commercial pet foods." *Genetic Toxicology and Environmental Mutagenesis*, Mutation Research 539 (2003) 195–201.

10. Kinze: 195.

CHAPTER 10

1. FDA, Center for Veterinary Medicine. Communications Staff, HFV-12, March 12, 2003.

2. Elizabeth Wiese., "Animal-feed investigation leads to dioxin tests in two states." *USA Today*, March 26, 2003.

3. Center for Veterinary Medicine. *FDA Veterinarian*, May/June 2003. 12–13.

4. Raloff, Janet. "New PCBS?" *Science News*, October 25, 2003. 266.

CHAPTER 11

1. Arlian, Larry, Schumann, Jeffrey, Morgan, Marjorie, Glass, Robert. "Serum

immunoglobulin E against storage mite allergens in dogs with atopic dermatitis." *AMJR,* Vol. 64, No. 1, January 2003. 32.

2. Sing, Mitchell. Veterinary dermatologist (ACVD) in Phoenix, Arizona on Veterinary Information Network, 2004.

3. White, Patricia. "Update on Canine food Allergy." Western Veterinary Conference. February 2003.

4. Yamashita K, Fujiwara C, Azuma R, Sawazaki T, Nakao Y, Hasegawa A. "Determination of antigenic proteins of housedust mites in 90 dogs suffering from Atopic Dermatitis." *Journal of Veterinary Medical Science* 64[8]: 673–6 August 2002

5. Food Standards Agency, Department of Health, UK. "Storage mites in Foodstuffs." No. 96, October 1996. http://archive.food.gov.uk/maff/archive/infosheet/1996/no96/96mites.htm

6. Arlian, et a.l 32.

7. Emmanuel Bensignor and Didier N. Carlotti. "Sensitivity Patterns to House Dust Mites and Forage Mites in Atopic Dogs: 150 Classes." *Veterinary Dermatology* February 2002. 13[1]: 37–42.

8. *Encyclopedia Britannica* s.v. "Fungus" 2003 . January 28, 2003."

9. Money, Nicholas P. "The Mysterious world of mushrooms, molds, and mycotoxins." *Mr. Bloomfield's Orchard* , Oxford University Press, 2002. 170.

10. Banwart: 170.

11. Council for Agricultural Science and Technology, Ames, Iowa, USA *Mycotoxins: Risks in Plant, Animal and Human Systems,* January 2003. 4.

12. CAST: 143.

13. Proctor, D.L, ed. "Grain storage techniques, evolution, and trends in deveoping countries," Consultant FAO Agricultural Services Bulletin No. 109GASCA—Group for Assistance on Systems Relating to Grain after Harvest Food Food and Agriculture Organization of the United Nations (FAO) Rome, 1994. http://www.fao.org/docrep/T1838E/T1838E00/htm# Contents

14. Hughes: "overt..." 700.

15. Jones, Hunt and King. *Veterinary Pathology,* Lippincott Williams & Wilkens, 1997. 540.

16. Chafee and Himes. "Aflatoxicosis in Dogs." *American Journal of Veterinary Research.* Vol. 30, No. 10, October 1969. 1748

17. Bingham, Phillips, and Bauer. "Potential for the dietary protection against

the effects of aflatoxins in animals." *Journal of the American Veterinary Medical Accociation*, Vol. 22, No. 5. March 1, 2003. 593.

18. Pitt, John and Hocking, Ailsa. "Food Science Australia." from *Mycotoxin Monthly*, Vol. 5, No. 8.

19. *Petfood Industry* Magazine 1995 37(6), 37–38.

20. CAST: 62.

21. CAST: 86.

22. CAST: 105.

23. Hughes, Graham & Grieb. "Overt Signs of Toxicity to Dogs and Cats of Dietary Deoxynivalenol." *Journal of Animal Sciences*, 1999. 693.

24. CAST: 104.

25. Mareth, Ed. "Ultra-premium ingredients." Pet Food Forum 2003. Also personal conversations with feed grain suppliers.

26. CAST: 110.

27. Hughes: 699.

28. CAST: 110.

29. CAST: 111.

30. North Carolina State University Mycotoxin Laboratory http://www.ces.ncsu.edu/gaston/staff/pdrechsl/mycotoxins/mycodata.html Accessed October, 2002

31. CAST: 103.

32. Bondy, Pestka. "Immunomodulation by Fungal Toxins." *Journal of Toxicology and Environmental Health, Part B*. 2000. 3: 130.

33. Banwart: 319.

34. Hughes, Graham & Grieb. "Evaluation of the potential adverse influence of vomitoxin (DON) on palatability and consumption of dogs and cats." *Proceedings of the Petfood Forum*, 1998. 141.

35. Hughes, Graham & Grieb. "Overt Signs of Toxicity to Dogs and Cats of Dietary Deoxynivalenol," *Journal of Animal Sciences*, 1999, Vol. 77. 693–700.

36. Splittstoesser, D.F. and King, A.D. Jr. "Enumeration of Byssochlamys and Other Heat Resistant Molds." in Compendium. 205.

37. Hughes: "Overt....." 699–700.

38. CAST: 48.

39. CAST: 58.

40. Bondi: 113.

41. Harvard Medical School's Consumer Health Information website, www.intelihealth.com "Scientists Find Clue to Carcinogen." October 3, 2002.

PART FOUR

1. Vaupel, Carey, Christiensen. "It's Never Too Late." *Journal of Science,* Vol. 301 September 19, 2003. 1679–1680.

2. Abbott, Alison. "Gut Reaction." *Nature,* Vol. 427, January 22, 2004. 284–285.

CHAPTER 12

1. University of South Florida, Health Science Center. "Antioxidant-rich Diets improve age-related declines in mental function of rats." USF/VA researchers report, July 15, 2002.

2. Egner et al. "Chlorophyllin Intervention and Carcinogenesis." Oxford University Press. Vol. 19, 1323–1326, 1998; and Harttig and Bailey. "Chemo-protection by natural chlorophylls in vivo: inhibition of dibenzo[a,l]pyrene-DNA adducts in rainbow trout liver."

3. Mosaad A, Abdel-Wahhab, and Soher E. Aly. "Antioxidants and Radical Scavenging Properties of Vegetable Extracts in Rats Fed Aflatoxin-Contaminated Diet." *Journal of Agricultural and Food Chemistry,* 2003. 51, 2409–2414.

4. Egner et al. "Chlorophyllin intervention reduces aflatoxin-DNA adducts in individuals at high risk for liver cancer." *Proceedings of the National Academy of Sciences* ISA, Vol. 98, Issue 25, December 4, 2001 14601–14606.

5. J.F.V. Vincent. "Texture of plants and fruits." *Feeding and the Texture of Food,* Cambridge University Press, 1999. 21–25.

6. From private conversations with Dr. Ken Hildebrand, marine biologist at Oregon State University, Corvalis, Oregon, and Dr. James Morris, University of California at Davis. September 2000.

7. Lord, Richard, and Bralley, J. Alexander. "Polyunsaturated Fatty Acid-Induced Antioxidant Insufficiency." *Integrative Medicine,* Vol. 1, No. 1, December 2002. 38.

8. Personal conversations and observation, and from Veterinary Information Network, Atopic Dermatitis update, January 2004. Four of the nine participating veterinarians found some benefits from omega-3 fatty acids.

9. Joshi, Rao, Golwilkar, Patwardham, and Bhonde. "Fish Oil Supplementation of Rats during Pregnancy Reduces Adult Disease Risks in Their Offspring." *Journal of Nutrition,* Vol. 233, Issue 10, October 2003. 3170–3174.

10. *Journal Allergy Clinical Immunology,* December 2003; 112 (6) 1178–1184.

11. Raloff, J. "Calcium may become a dieter's best friend." *Science News,* April 29, 2000.

12. Dunn, T. J. personal correspondence and www.thepetcenter.com/xra/bone comp.html

13. Vallejo, Tomas-Barberan and Garcia-Viguera. "Phenolic compound contents in edible parts of broccoli inflorescences after domestic cooking." *Journal of the Science of Food and Agriculture* 83, issue 14, October 2003. 1511–1516.

14. Willett, Walter and Stampfer, Meir. Letters, *Scientific American,* May 2003. 14–15.

15. National Toxicology Program, National Institute of Health, alpha-chaconine and alpha-solanine, review of toxicological literature. http://ntp-server. niehs.nih.gov/htdocs/Chem_Background/ExecSumm/ChaconineSolanine/ch ac_91.html#toxdata.

16. Means, Charlotte. "The Wrath of Grapes." ASPCA Animal Watch, Summer 2002. Vol. 22, No. 2.

17. The American Society for the Prevention of Cruelty to Animals, Animal Poison Control Center, "Organic mulch fertilizer may pose hazard to dogs." March 2003.

CHAPTER 13

1. Bingham et al. "Potential for dietary proetction against the effects of aflatoxins in animals." *JAVMA* 222, No. 5, March 2003. 592

2. Petfood Industry E-newsletter, June 3, 2003. From AC Homescan Consumer Facts 2002 Report.

3. Cramer, Cindy. "Hidden Killers in Dog Food." *The Whole Dog Journal,* July 2000. Cramer lists trembling, irrational fear, and avoidance of bright light as some of the strange behavior experienced by her dog after consumption of low levels of aflatoxin-contaminated dry dog food.

4. CAST: 15.

5. Young, Kristin. "Tremorgenic Mycotoxin Intoxication with Penitrem A and Roquefortine in Two Dogs." *Journal of the American Veterinary Mediical Association* 222[1]:52–53 Jan 1 '03. Case Report: Schell, Mary, ASPCA National Animal Poison Control Center. "Mycotoxin Intoxication." *Veterinary Med* 95[4]: April 2000. 285-286. *Toxicology Brief;* and personal conversations.

CHAPTER 14

1. Kerns, Nancy. "Toxic Lawns." *The Whole Dog Journal*, Belvoir Publications, Inc. May 2001. 4–6.
2. Raloff, Janet. "New PCBS. Throughout life, our bodies accumulate flame retardants, and scientists are starting to worry." *Science News*, October 25, 2003. 266.

CHAPTER 15

1. Dudley, Kathleen "Are 'Spot-On' Flea Killers Safe?" Journal of the American Holistic Veterinary Medical Association, January 2003 Vol. 21, No. 4. 33.

CHAPTER 16

1. Lane, Mark. "The serious search for an anti-aging pill," *Scientific American* August 2002. 36.
2. Calle, Rodriguez, Walker-Thurmond, and Thun "Overweight, Obesity, and Mortality from Cancer in a Prospectively Studies Cohort of US Adults." *The New England Journal of Medicine*, Vol. 348: 1625–1638. April 24, 2003.
3. Sears, Barry. *The Omega Rx Zone*, ReganBooks 2002. 59–60.
4. Kealy, Richard et al. "Effects of diet restriction on life span and age-related changes in dogs." *Journal of the American Veterinary Mediical Association*, Vol. 220, No. 9, May 1, 2002. 1315–1320.
5. Gorman, James. "Survival of the Fattest: How Pets Got So Big." *NY Times*, Sept. 16, 2003. Gorman references studies by Nestle Purina and Hills Pet Nutrition.
6. Shell, Ellen Ruppel. *The Hungry Gene. The Science of Fat and the Future of Thin*, Atlantic Monthly Press, New York 2002. 173–183. Shell reviews the work of Dr. David Barker and his long term studies of the Dutch Hunger Winter 1944–1945.
7. Vaupel, James W., Carey, James R., and Christensen, Kaare. "Aging: It's Never Too Late." *Science*, Sept. 19, 2003. 301: 1679–1681.
8. Anson, Guo, de Cabo, Iyun, Rios, Hagepanos, Ingram, Lane and Mattson. "Intermittent fasting dissociates beneficial effects of dietary restriction on glucose metabolism and neuronal resistance to injury from caloric intake." *Proceedings of the National Academy of Sciences*, Online Early Edition, April 28, 2003. www.pnas.org/cgi/doi/10.1073/pnas.1035720100.
9. Coppinger: 169.

10. Center, Sharon. "Obesity Prevention." *Petfood Industry*, January 2003.
11. R.J.Rose and M.S. Bloomberg. "Responses to sprint exercise in the greyhound: effects on haematology, serum biochemistry and muscle metabolites." *Research in Veterinary Science*, 1989, 47. 212–218.

CHAPTER 17
1. Blaxter: 194.

APPENDIX C
1. Bourdon, Richard M. *Understanding Animal Breeding*, Second Edition, Prentice-Hall, 2000. 25.
2. Padgett,DVM, George. *Control of Canine Genetic Diseases*, Howell Book House, 1999. 191.
3. For an excellent discussion on the evolution of dogs, the authors recommend *Dogs: A Startling New Understanding of Canine Origin, Behavior, & Evolution* by Ray and Lorna Coppinger. Scribner, 2001.
4. Hare, Brown, Williamson, Tomasello. "The Domestication of Social Cognition in Dogs." *Science,* Vol. 298, November 22, 2002. 1634–1636.
5. Miklosi, A, Kubinyl, Tpal, Gacsi, Viranyl and Csanyyi. "A Simple Reason for a Big Difference: Wolves Do Not Look Back at Humans, but Dogs Do." *Current Biology*, Vol. 13, April 29, 2004. 763–766.
6. Wilcox and Walkowicz. *Atlas of Dog Breeds of the World*, T.F.H. Publications, 1989. 334, 450.
7. Only a few breeds are considered non-shedding. It is often stated that non-shedders have a continuously growing hair cycle, though the scientific understanding of this is limited. *Small Animal Dermatology*, Muller, Kirk, and Scott, W.B. Saunders, 1989. 4–7.
8. Whitney DVM, Leon. *How to Breed Dogs*, Howell Book House, 1971. 159.
9. Scott and Fuller. *Genetics and the Social Behavior of the Dog*, University of Chicago Press, 1965. 286.
10. Onstott, Kyle. *The New Art of Breeding Better Dogs*, Howell Book House, 1946. 145.

APPENDIX D
1. For those readers that want to explore this topic in much greater detail, we recommend *Plague Time, The new germ theory of disease*, by Paul Ewald. While

he focuses on humans, and the role of germs in diseases previously thought to be genetic, his arguments and mathematics hold for canine diseases as well. Anchor Books, 2002.

2. Wills, Malcomb B. *Genetics of the Dog,* Howell Book House 1989. 33–336.

3. Smith et al. "Evaluation of Risk Factors for Degenerative Joint Disease Associated With Hip Dysplasia in German Shepherd Dogs, Golden Retrievers, Labrador Retrievers and Rottweilers." *JAVMA,* 219 (12) December 15, 2001. 1719–1724.

4. An example: a recent study with humans tied testicular cancer to a fetus' pollutant contact. Contact with certain hormone-like chemicals before birth raises a male's risk of various genital problems. (*Science News,* Jan 11 03, Vol. 163. 22. From Environmental Health Perspectives)

5. Haney, Daniel. Reporting in the Washington Post March 7, 2003 on presentation at Johns Hopkins University, American Heart Association meeting March 2003.

6. Shell: 173–190

7. From Dr. David Barker's web site, Fetal Origins of Adult Disease Division http://www.som.soton.ac.uk/research/foad/barker.asp

8. *The Economist,* Vol. 367, No 8328, June 14, 2003. 78.

9. Barker, David and Lackland, Daniel. "Prenatal Influences on Stroke Mortality in England and Wales." *Stroke, Journal of the American Heart Association,* June 19, 2003.

10. Shell: 179.

11. Ridley, Matt. *Nature via Nurture,* HarperCollins Publishers, 2003. 154–157.

12. Ridley, Matt. 156.

13. Pottenger, Francis M. *Pottenger's Cats, A Study in Nutrition.* Price-Pottenger Nutrition Foundation, Inc. 2nd edition.

Request FREE information! (please check boxes that apply):

☐ Speaking/Seminars   ☐ Email Newsletter   ☐ Consulting

Please tell us about YOU! (we need to know where to send the goods):

Name _____

Address _____

City _____ State _____ Zip _____

Email address _____

Order more copies of See Spot Live Longer!

@ $14.95 each =   Subtotal _____

S&H _____ $ 4.95

if ordering more than 2 books,
please add an additional $2 per book   _____

Total _____

Please send Check or Money Order to: Creekobear Press
P.O. Box 50939
Eugene, OR 97405

Credit card orders and requests may be made through our website:
www.seespotlivelonger.com

*Quantity discounts are available on bulk purchases of this book for
educational and training purposes. For information, write to us at our
address above, or email us through our website. Thank you!*